Beats, Hippies and Native Americans

Stephen M. Catchpole

ISBN:8799579960
ISBN-13:9788799579969

DEDICATION

Take the train from Casablanca going south.

This book is dedicated to the music of the 1960's.

CONTENTS

ACKNOWLEDGMENTS

Cover photo: American maid is five foot tall in blue.

1. Introduction

Many people who grew up during the sixties look back on that decade with an affinity to the music and events that happened then. Almost forty years later I found myself looking for a history module and a thesis to complete a history degree that had lay dormant while my kids grew up filed under; *'one of these days'* or *'when the time is right'*. But as most people know the time is never right unless unforeseen developments kick in like they did with me in 2008.[1] I found myself reluctantly walking up the line at the university administration office to see what modules were being offered. I was thinking Roman History or maybe First World War poetry, bury my head in books for a year and get it over with. You could have knocked me over with a feather when my eyes fell on the title: 'Rock Military Style – A phenomenon on the fringe of politics, culture, ethics and visual memory'. What's going on here? Someone is pulling my chain; everyone knows that Academia is the sacred realm of the living dead! And they who walk its hallowed halls will find no pleasure there, only sorrow and human despair lurking in the shadows. What I was not aware of was that as the first decade of the new millennium was drawing to a close, the role of popular music in the sixties was starting to gain academic recognition. For young and old students some attractive areas for research had started to open up. Whereas previously you had to blow the dust of some book about Oliver Cromwell and wander around a soggy field in Naseby to get some understanding. Now you had the possibility of putting some vinyl on the turntable and lying on the sofa to try and understand what the attraction of the sixties was all about. History was being made in 2009 when Hope University in Liverpool offered a MA on the Beatles which according to Dr. Mike Brocken was the first of its kind in the world. By coincidence this was exactly the time I had the opportunity to finish my History degree. My reluctance was starting to fade as I signed up for the course. After finishing a very enlightening module that resulted in my assignment on Jimi Hendrix and his Rock Military Style it was full steam ahead. Inspired by Rock Artists wearing military Jackets I decided to focus my thesis on Neil Young and his use of Comanche War Shirts as they were military symbols for the Native Americans. These war shirts were military uniforms used in exactly the same way Europeans used the military uniforms in combat. Many artists like Hendrix, Country Joe, Clapton and others bands had adopted the 'military look' as part of their image during the sixties. The other dimension I found interesting was Neil Young's use of Native American artifacts in his work that bought the theme into public the public eye. This created mainstream awareness of Native American culture that could have helped contribute to the plight of the Native Americans and their struggle for civil rights groups during that period. This book is an extension of my research on Neil Young[2] combined with a summary of the events that happened during the period that cut the 20th century right in half.

While doing my research I created what I call a:

Neil Young History Tree.

This comprises of what was around while he was growing up?

What were the events that influenced him and others during that time? How deep do the roots of the tree go?

I was especially interested in the history of the Native Americans and how they had been portrayed in Western Culture.

What were on those branches in 1966 when he formed a band with Stephen Stills in L.A.? Beatles? Civil Rights Movement? Hippies?

It was all there growing in the tree. Some branches close by and others far away but all connected and feeding from mother earth through the roots and breathing through the leaves.

The main focus is on his work in that period particularly with Buffalo Springfield and on Native Americans. How they were portrayed in films and represented in our culture. It is the duty of teachers, amateur family historians, school classes and others to document periods in history while the people who lived through that period are still alive. If you want to write about a band from back then try and find someone in your family who saw them and interview them. Write it down for prosperity, tell your grandchildren about it, put it online. If you are serious about doing something like this either as a classroom assignment or as an independent research project it is important to start with one piece of hard evidence for example a family photograph from the period or a primary source like an album cover.

I have tried to focus my research on specific areas and one of the main ones is the visual record of Neil's use of Native American imagery on album covers, photographs, films, tour posters (from the period and contemporary ones.) Written works about Neil Young: biographies, sleeve notes, magazine articles and internet web sites like 'Thrasher', 'Rust List' and CSN&Y 'Lee Shore' , these are internet discussion groups and websites where fans of Neil Young and CSN&Y exchange information and stay connected. I still had to bury my head in books for a year but the soundtrack was pretty amazing and present day DVDs are a dream for researchers as many are accompanied by interviews and extra materials. Basically in the 'Halls of the Dead' they have a formula where you narrow everything down by 'killing off your darlings' and finishing up with a nice little academic thesis that make all the wise men nod in agreement.

As I was working alone I decided to avoid going down that route and I expanded the theme to include other areas. Things that I thought would shed more light on the subject and show how historical events converged and influenced developments in society at a given time. Describing the convergences that created the sixties is no mean task and I don't propose that this book adequately does that. However one of the main objects of the research was to try and find documentation and give references to some of the events of the period that are in some way connected and converged into the mainstream. Particularly in connection with Neil Young and what was going on at the time. Another side effect I hope to achieve is jogging the memory banks of some the older readers and inspires younger readers to investigate more about the decade that had such a defining role in the shaping of the 20th century.

In the best scenario some of the associations I have drawn will encourage the reader to link certain areas with things they would not normally associate with each other. These connections should help in interpreting the events that occurred at that time. There is no denying the influence the 1960's had on the generation that lived through it or how that generation influenced the decades that followed. They even seem to have influenced old age! Being in your sixties today is no longer considered as old as it was in 1960. Many of that generation are still very creative and young at heart; people like Neil Young are living proof of that. My own background for this research was that I was a big fan of Neil Young's work from that period and I have followed his career loosely from the side-lines since then. I had strange bouts of Déjà Vu during the research as I recognized old magazine covers and articles that I might have read at the time. Things that had somehow got logged on and then downloaded into my mind. Now all these years later familiar images resurfaced that I must have passed on newsstands in London.

I had seen Neil Young and the Santa Monica Flyers in concert during the early seventies[3] and decided to see him again in Berlin in 2006 to see if he can still deliver the goods. I have to say during the first acoustic set he held the auditorium enthralled and during the electric second half he blew them away. The climax was the encore; 'Keep on Rocking in the Free World' the sentiment was not lost on an audience in a city that until recently had been encircled by the Berlin Wall.

For those of us who grew up in the 1960's The Beatles and Rolling Stones was standard issue for all. Artists like Neil Young, Leonard Cohen and to some extent Bob Dylan came under personal effects. Without doubt the music and events of the 60's left a profound effect on the way we live and think today. Many people who lived through those years (or people like me who caught the tail end of the decade) were not really aware how significantly life changing these events would become. Many people probably thought the changes were not going to last and the society would eventually return to the post war authoritarian regimes. But fortunately that did not happen. So many events from that decade rise to the surface when we make assessments of the 20th century. Despite the fact I was barely a teenager in the mid-sixties I was old enough to appreciate that this was a time of immense creativity and radical change. For me (and many others) it was popular music that made the biggest impression against a media backdrop of Swinging London. Harold Wilson, Concorde, CND and Northern Ireland combined with outside influences mainly from the US of Kennedy and anti-war demonstrations projected by newsreels from Vietnam, race riots and the Space Race. The sixties was a time when economic growth, technological progress and creative progress seemed to go hand in hand as they went from strength to strength. This is one of the main differences with the sixties compared to the other decades; the social aspects (and to some extent the hedonistic elements) and the technical developments had equal prominence in what was going on. On the one hand technical progress where the machines were becoming more sophisticated (computers were slowly gaining prominence but nothing like we know today). On the other hand there was a growing concern among young people that the human condition and the quality of life and our social interaction were diminishing. Although these two elements (technical and social) had very different goals and attracted very different types of people they also interacted with each other and you cannot present the sixties without considering both of them. As time went by these two types merged closer together and people became generally looser and more relaxed. No one wanted to appear square, uptight, old fashioned and out of touch. The rigidness in the society started to change and young people were the driving force.

It was a time of social change that helped change moral values that in turn influenced fashion styles (or vice versa, depending how you look at it) . These changes of attitudes and outlooks were helped along by emerging pop groups. These groups contributed vastly to the resolution and feel good factor among the younger generation and facilitated the colouring of Britain from the drab grey matter of the post war years to a vibrant society. It was this chain reaction of events that appeared to be unrelated to each other that somehow created the fusion that formed the decade that became an inspiration to so many. If music and events staged by the counter culture changed the norms of how young people saw themselves personally i.e. changed their views of themselves as human beings and their outlook on life. That in turn affected their attitude to the external things in their lives like war and racism?

Many groups and artists like Neil Young, Bob Dylan, the Beatles, Stones and Jimi Hendrix had instrumental roles in this development. In the UK it was the Beatles in 1963 that kick started the whole process of the sixties literally confronting an archaic, authoritarian, drab grey Britain and leading the way to creating an exciting and stimulating place for young people to grow up in. The Beatles were to Britain what Bob Dylan was to American in helping to revitalize youth and let them be young! It was almost as if before the fifties and sixties, there was no such thing as a teenager! Young people were just mirror images of adults waiting to get old. One must remember that the post war years in Britain were especially hard for ordinary working people. They had become some of Europe's poorest, with inner city slums and with war widows pensions way below the ones of their German counterparts.

The British people had shared the burden of the war with the Americans but they did not share wonderful post war years of prosperity that America enjoyed. Rationing in the UK lasted up until 4th July 1954 when John Lennon had just turned 13. No wonder the Beatles found American prosperous on their initial visits compared to England where even the sunshine seemed to be rationed. In the wake of the Beatles success and musical innovation hundreds of bands formed in the UK to accommodate the insatiable growing market for the new Beat Music. The inspiration for these bands came from the other side of the Atlantic and was a potpourri of Jazz, Big band music and African American inspired music like Soul, Blues and Rock and Roll. Bands known as Skiffle groups like John Lennon's Quarrymen found a major inspiration in Country and Western music and later bands on both sides of the Atlantic became influenced by folk music artists like Bob Dylan.

Generally speaking many of the UK bands like the Beatles and the Stones were influenced by the Chicago Blues. Whereas many American bands in the sixties Buffalo Springfield included evolved from Folk Music and this has given very distinctive differences in styles. The swinging sixties as they became known evolved during the Space Age. That generation of creative people got caught up in an atmosphere that anything was possible as Astronauts left the stratosphere in spaceships reaching for other planets. There was a profound feeling of optimism among the young people who suddenly found they were riding on a wave of the economic prosperity and unforeseen technical advancement. The sixties heralded in the space age and its mission statement of finding new frontiers and putting a man on the moon. The space age terminology spread to other areas, guitars were given names like Stratocaster and Telecaster. Ideas became "far out" as people got "high" and became "spaced out". In 1962 Joe Meeks produced the song 'Telstar'[4] by the British group the Tornadoes it hit the airwaves five weeks after the communications satellite of the same name was launched. This single reached number one on both sides of the Atlantic. Featuring the Clavioline it heralded distinctive sound of the space age. The single was backed by a song called 'Jungle fever' giving the buyer both ends of the spectrum. In design "modern, high tech and state of the art" became buzz words in an industry that was shaping the appearance of the decade as can been seen in the designs of almost everything down from architecture of buildings to cars and planes. As the sixties advanced the artists' innovation was encouraged by the technical progress that had become available.

One big invention in the area of sound was the transistor which revolutionized radios not only in size but also availability. Popular music was in the vanguard as bands pushed the boundaries of what could be achieved in the studio by using untraditional methods and synthesizers combined with more exotic instruments like the sitar. A major breakthrough was the incredible guitar sound of Jimi Hendrix suddenly over the airways we heard an intergalactic audio experience that was fit to accompany mankind's first moonwalk. This is one of the great failings in the sixties that despite all the creativity going on all around the globe the priorities of man's journey into space was still governed by the conservative powers that be. In many areas they chose not take chances but took the safe route of time long traditions. We did not send up any "space cadets" in the Pink Floyd sense of the term, no-one got high on the moon instead we sent engineers and military people. The astronauts did however look slightly hip when they returned and stood on the ship decked out in shades, beard stubbles, and wide grins. Writers like Hunter Thompson who could have transcribed the experience so people would have been able to share it were still considered a disruptive force. Even though he had been trained by the Air Force he could not be trusted at the controls of a space craft. The entertainment industry still got inspiration from the event and did what it could to represent it; rock bands like the Pink Floyd wrote numbers like "Interstellar Overdrive" which took the listeners musical experience to a higher level of awareness. Young people listened to albums like 'Ummagumma' in darkened rooms to get the mind expanding experience of a live concert. The real experience would have been accompanied by a psychedelic light show. Films like '2001 a Space Odyssey' released in 1968 depicted man mastering outer space accompanied by strikingly effective soundtrack of classical music by Johan Strauss. This experience was for many of the working class in the British audience their first exposure to a long classical music session. Stanley Kubrick also used pioneering special effects that really knocked people out (loaded or unloaded). The sixties became a new age where everyone seemed to be pushing the envelope not least fashion designers like Mary Quant and Nigel Weymouth. Bringing flamboyant colour and making London swing they opened shops like: 'Lord Kitchener's Valet' (1964), 'Bazaar' (1965), 'Granny Takes a Trip' (1966). The first Kitchener's Valet shop in the Portobello Road took inspiration from the Lord Kitchener 'Your Country Needs You' recruitment poster and the military dress styles from the previous century. Peter Blake said that he and Paul McCartney were walking past the shop when they got the inspiration for the Sargent Pepper LP cover. Lord Kitchener's Valet was the favourite shop of many bands like Hendrix, The Beatles, The Stones, Cream and The Who to name just a few[5]. The store closed in 1977 but remains an icon of Swinging London.

There was an unprecedented government spending by the labour government during this period to improve the conditions and living standards of ordinary people in Britain. This was sometimes initiated by the Trade Unions who had become more powerful but generally working class people wanted more out of life and started to demand it. Especially young people like the 18 year old dramatist Shelagh Delaney who wrote the play "A Taste of Honey"[6] made into a film in 1961. "A Taste of Honey" took up themes like race, class, gender and sexual orientation that were still taboo in Britain in the middle of the twentieth century. The film depicts the young 17 year old working class girl called Jo growing up in Salford. She wants to go to Art School but becomes pregnant with her black merchant seaman boyfriend who then sails away. The prospect single mother is befriended by Geoff a gay Art Student who moves in the flat with her. In the opening sequence after the mother and Jo do a runner from a bedsit, Jo rides on a bus through Salford, past images of the grandeur of the British Empire captured in the architecture and statues of Queen Victoria, the Crimean War and First World War. One cannot fail to see contrast of past glories to modern working class gloom and Jo's humble existence and the drabness of her life in a Northern city. Five years later Ken Loach's film for Play for Today 'Cathy Come Home'[7] had the same effect in increasing peoples social awareness of the appalling housing conditions and highlighted the desolate future many young couples had to face. Alongside all this creativity and atmosphere of rebellious youth, the voice of dissent for social changes was becoming louder. People started to question the authority and wisdom of their governments on a massive scale and in a way previously unseen in the West. The social change was so immense that in the middle of the twentieth century the old world order that had been struggling to maintain the status quo since the end of WW2 finally succumbed. Empires crumbled as colonies gained independence and the streets of the capitols of the Western World became filled with people fighting and protesting about their countries involvement in external wars like Vietnam and Biafra. This was a big change from the previous decade when the Korean War that was fought virtually without challenge from the general public even though the dynamics and end result were very similar to those of the Vietnam War. In the sixties youth culture and civil rights groups wanted radical changes and protested to end the war in Vietnam and the use and manufacture of nuclear weapons CND 'Ban the Bomb' started to make annual marches from London to Aldermaston. [8]

In America during the sixties there was segregation throughout the Southern States and African Americans all over America began fighting for equal rights. In towns like Montgomery in the South the discrimination was unbelievable right down to basic things like African Americans not only having to sit at the back of the bus but also having to vacate their seat for a white person if the bus became too full. They were also segregated in canteens and restaurants. Interracial marriages were a criminal offence in many States. People wanted change and started to demand it. The Women's Liberation Movement in the sixties started to challenge what was then a very male dominated world. They demanded equal rights and equal pay for women. Fully inspired by the times civil rights organizations flourished. Almost all minority groups, started getting some form of recognition and representation. It was clear that the new generation wanted their children to live in the world that was vastly different from the one that their parents had created for them. Angela Davis's mother said to her when she was a child, something along the lines of "this is how the world is but not how it should be"[9]

The Second World War had exposed large numbers of the male population (many of them from working class backgrounds) to exotic parts of the world, they would otherwise not have come into contact with. Here they experienced many different cultures, ideas and values. These experiences had a profound influence on these young men who had been destined to be coal miners, factory workers and farm labourers: Apart from the psychological impact of sometimes finding themselves in dangerous, far flung places, like Cairo or Singapore. They also faced the technological challenges of training for air crews, submarines and tanks. Weapons became more and more sophisticated and they had to prepare themselves for a much more demanding environment than that of ordinary manual labour. These experiences gave them a totally different perception of life during their formative years. These fathers of the sixties generation had a right to expect more of the future than the generation before them. Their fathers had also been through a war in the trenches and in the UK at least promised a

'Land fit for Heroes'. But in the end they returned to dole queues and unemployment or factories and mine pits if they were lucky.

American servicemen were fortunate in having the GI Bill created by the US government for their returning soldiers after WW2. This bill gave them the chance to take an education and make a very different kind of future for themselves. They were able to utilize their individual personal changes that the military experience had given them. Again there were no such possibilities for the working class Brits who had served. They went back to manual labour jobs or had their army discharge delayed so they could be used to try and reclaim parts of the British Empire like Malaya from various groups who wanted independence. Many of these colonies had been occupied by the Japanese during the war. Now the war was over the British, French and Dutch wanted them to voluntarily return to colonial status! It seems incredible today but that is how people thought back then. Burma, Ceylon, Malaysia and India are British and should continue to be ruled by Britain. However if you have been a resistance fighter and thrown one foreign power out, you don't quite share that view. You start to think why should we be ruled by anyone?

For the civilian population in central Europe the war had left a legacy of a massive upheaval. Alone in West Germany there were 11 million displaced homeless people. There were vast vacuums throughout the industrial nations for equipment and products. Tokyo had been firebombed in much the same style as Dresden and Berlin. Two of Japans major cities lay in nuclear ruins. American industry was rapidly filling the vacuum which boosted the American economy to unprecedented heights. Since the end of WW2 various governments especially those with colonies like Britain and France tried to return to the prestige and eminence they had before the war. But this was not to be, the two ageing European World Powers who had enjoyed such prosperous heydays during the previous century now fought hard to try and maintain some form of control over their dwindling colonies and Empires. After Suez, Britain and France finally had to give up any pretense of being 'World Powers'. They now stepped aside to let the new Super Powers, American and The Soviet Union dictate to the rest of world a New World Order. The world became bi polar and would remain so for the next 50 years. While all this was taking place the children who had been born in the aftermath of war grew into teenagers. In Britain and American this new generation wanted something different and the Beatles gave it to them. Everyone living in the sixties and listening to popular music with the Beatles in the vanguard would have to agree with Mike Brocken that the music we remember has a leading role in our development at the time we hear it and becomes a big part of our identity, in many ways it defines who we are. "Musical memory has a power of its own. Moreover, musical taste and experience are closely linked to personality and emotion. The music we remember is, without exaggeration, part of who we are."[10] Mike Broken goes on to say "If you look at popular music generally and the Beatles specifically they are issues about identity. If you think about how important popular music is from an identity point of view. People create their own identities and ideas about themselves more often than not with some kind of music or art form, creating is an essential part of that and that identity then creates audiences who respond in a certain way. And that music is mediated through systems so you can see a developmental area of study that one thing leads into something else which is very important to people". [11]

Simply put this means that the music we hear in our youth contributes to our development during our formative years and helps to form us into whom we become as adults. Some people reject this side of themselves and others cultivate it and carry musical memories throughout their lives in the material form of LPs and cassettes probably now replaced by digitally audited versions on CD. By listening to this music they can return to that time in their minds and recall events that meant something to them then. The loyal ageing fans might turn up for gigs when their favourite bands reform for a nostalgic retro-tour. In this way they try and achieve some of the sensation of the thrill and unity they felt back then. By this I do not propose they are locked in time. We all listen to other music and our musical tastes change and develop but we keep the music from the formative years in a corner of our mind or bookcase to take out and reflect on from time to time.

I was 13 years old during the 1967 'Summer of Love,' and witnessed what was going on from the side-lines, absorbing the atmosphere and especially the music that was dominating the airways. Sixteen and seventeen year olds would have experienced the period in a much more liberating way. I could appreciate the music but not always understand the double meanings.

For me the commercially big hit singles from groups like Peter Green's Fleetwood Mac, Syd Barrett's Pink Floyd, Cream and Traffic seemed to point in another direction from the standard Rock and Roll songs, towards a more transcendental peaceful and mellow existence. This sounds quite corny now but if you listen to Cream's "Badge "or Traffic's "Paper Sun" or Fleetwood Mac's "Albatross" you might get the gist of what I mean. Personally Fleetwood Mac's hauntingly sorrowful 'Man of the World' had a profound effect on me.

Later songs like Joni Mitchells 'Big Yellow Taxi' and Neil Young's 'Heart of Gold' really showed the power of the human voice accompanied by an acoustic guitar. These sounds of intelligent pop coming out of my tranny filled the airwaves in the morning as I got ready for work. Everyone over 50 has a lot of personal knowledge and experience to various aspects of the sixties. Like millions of others I was definitely influenced by the musical vibe that ran through that period. The volatile combinations of different lifestyles and the attitude of the rebellious youth groups began effecting elements in the society that changed many peoples outlook on life. The sixties was a pretty potent experience for any impressionable adolescent growing up and it was that group of young people who were targeted. As the jazz musician and social commentator George Melly stated:

"The sixties downfall was that it did not include everyone, it was only for the young".

To a certain degree when looking specifically at what is called The Sixties Revolution, this is true. However the social changes like being able to rent a flat with your girlfriend and developments in the music world ran right across the spectrum and affected everyone. This is evident in the music charts in 1968 where the diversity of the music shows that it was not only the youth that were buying records and having a good time.

Many older people were bewildered by what was happening around them. But many younger parents did try and tune in and loosen up a bit, especially towards the close of the decade. Films like the Graduate[12] helped them to keep abreast with what was going on and the music by Simon and Garfunkel pushed the Beatles 'White Album' out of the number one chart position.

To put the sixties into some sort of historical perspective 50 years have now passed since then and we are starting to appreciate the fact that the generation that grew up then is slowly starting to die out. We have to make an effort to focus on the era if we are going to get sufficient first-hand accounts. One problem is many people have trouble in viewing the period and anything to do with popular entertainment as 'serious history.' My own attitude towards writing about this period and putting it into a historical context is best illustrated by what I remember as a child growing up in Britain. How did I view historical events at the start of the sixties? For example when I was about six years old the Second World War had been over for 15 years and I grew up watching black and white TV shows like, 'All Our Yesterdays'. These TV documentaries made that period seem like ancient history.

How do young people relate to the sixties today? Do they watch a film like 'Making Woodstock' or 'The Boat that Rocked' and think "Wow! Things were really primitive back then, no iPods, no mobiles, how did people manage to keep in touch with each other with each other?" There is a wave of contemporary films with Beatle themes like 'Backbeat',' Nowhere Boy' and 'Across the Universe'. With these films it is possible to still get some comments about their historical accuracy from the surviving Beatles. Paul McCartney said that it was inaccurate to portray him without a leather jacket in the film 'Backbeat' There are also the two original Beatles films "Hard Day's Night" and "Help" that can be used as primary sources they reflect the attitudes and conditions that existed in England at that time. Many new films about the sixties are trying to describe some of these facts and events in the form of a story to describe a period in the transition from one age to another. The child / parent relationship described by the Beatles in the song 'She's Leaving Home' is very apparent for the UK just as Neil Young's 'Sugar

Mountain'[13] gives the North American view of growing up and moving out. These influences and the different events going on at the time had a major role in the forming of the ideals and values that people growing up started live by. Neil Young is credited with being a prominent influence in the sixties and continued during the subsequent decades to be a major artist that reached (and continues to reach) a large number of people through his music and work. I have covered his work more in depth in part two of this trilogy.[14] What follows now are observations about events and things that led to the sixties. With some emphasis on Native Americans, due to the fact I was collecting material about them for the thesis.

2. The First Americans, Beats, Hippies and the Counter Culture

To try and set the scene of how some of the events of the sixties came about I would like to point to some of the major contributors, like the emergence of the "Beat Poets" as a legitimate force. Allen Ginsberg released the poem 'Howl' in 1955 that was a seminal event that reached a wider audience and started to broaden people's outlook. In 1957 Ginsberg helped Jack Kerouac publish 'On the Road'. Before them, an inspiration and one generation older, William Burroughs had released 'Junkie' in 1952.

Then in the sixties Ginsberg worked together with Gary Snyder. Snyder was very much into promoting the Native American lifestyle and values, through events like the 'Gathering of the Tribes'. The Native American civil rights movement was formed and it ran parallel with the other civil rights movements during the sixties and early seventies, the outcome was a reassessment of the role of the Native American in America's history.

The role played by the film and entertainment industry in that process has been neglected and I hope to show that the exposure given by artists to the mainstream audience created an awareness that gradually put pressure on governments to change things not least the termination of the Vietnam War. This was a war where Native Americans and African Americans were represented in disproportioned numbers compared to Americans of European extraction.

As Buffalo Springfield member Ritchie Furay points out in his book "the Native American was the first of many personas deployed by Young throughout his career."[15] He was the Indian of the group in his Buffalo Springfield days before the phrase was coined. I have researched every major book on Neil Young and I have not come across more than a few paragraphs on the Native American style he used in the sixties. The main focus is naturally enough almost always on his music. This to me confirms that his visual image has been very much neglected by researchers. I have employed statements from people in memoirs or from documentaries and collections of essays as often as possible. In doing this I have tried to find some images of the period that will serve to transport the reader back in time and illustrate more clearly the points I am making. However when working with life histories of individual's people's recollections and memories are very selective from an unlimited number of possible memories people chose the ones that they see as contributing to their present identities that will collaborate with how they relate to others in the present.

Neil Young stated in the BBC documentary 'Don't Be Denied' quoting Dylan "I don't even know who that person is anymore who wrote those songs back then" Another aspect that contributes to how people react today when recalling some situations from 'back then' that have become sensitive i.e. tales of drunkenness and debauchery are obviously not good role models to give our kids. How do you expect them to study hard and get a career when Mum and Dad spent some years of their youth in the wilderness howling at the moon? For many people the sixties was a big wild party where having fun became the main goal. There is a tendency nowadays to tone that aspect of the decade down. With age comes maturity and people normally start to conform as the years pass. Understandably they do not want their own children to get involved in what is seen as extremely dangerous drugs compared to the ones around in the 1960s. This attitude is especially true concerning the way older people respond to questions about the sixties. There can be various reasons for this. On the one hand, the track record of a 'Rock Star' describing how he was totally Ga, Ga, during the sixties enhances his credibility; the same details of an individual now working in insurance or banking who led a 'wild life' in the sixties might not be so forthcoming for obvious reasons. Another thing that really struck me when I spoke to various people that were teenagers in the sixties was their reluctance to view that period as history. Veterans of a bygone era many still wearing T-shirts and jeans along with grey hair, find it hard to see themselves as living primary sources of an event that began more than half a century ago and it was hard for them to see their cherished LP's as 'historical artifacts'. To understand this point of view we have to appreciate that things have changed radically since that time in terms of being old. If you compare a sixty year old today with someone who is sixty in 1940 or 1960 you are in two very different universes. In regard to youth at that time I would propose similar parallels: The responsibilities of 16 and 17 year olds back then are similar to the responsibilities 20 to 21 year olds have today. Despite the fact that 20 years is not a very significant period of time in a historical context. Each twenty year period during the 20th century produced radical changes accelerated by two major wars. How life changed after the middle of century is quite phenomenal. These times have changed not only for the sixties generation many of whom are now starting to go on pension but also for the generations that followed them not least concerning education and choice of career. Just compare the opportunities a young person had in the first two decades of the twentieth century and compare them to the last two decades of those volatile hundred years where the Cold War ended and the Berlin Wall fell. For a kick off women had very few possibilities apart from getting married and raising a family. African Americans had few rights, Native Americans lived isolated on reservations run by whites. Being gay was Illegal. Then came the twentieth century that was shaped by huge events that would affect the rest of the century: revolution, dismantling of empires, two world wars, the constant threat of nuclear conflict, space exploration, countries divided by war and devastated by war and famine. Elements of all these things are contained in the sixties that besides being the halfway mark also became the hallmark for change.

The start of the twentieth century and a new age was signaled by the death of Queen Victoria on the 22nd January 1901. Her reign began on the 20th June 1837 and dominated the 19th century and became known as the Victorian age. When she died her eldest grandson Kaiser Wilhelm of Germany sat at her bedside and held her hand. While in America flags were flown at half-mast on President McKinley's orders.[16] Then 13 years later Wilhelm threw the world into disarray by declaring war on Russia and starting WW1. The real beginning of the age of technology had begun speeded along by the development of weapons needed for modern warfare. This necessitated a movement away from classical education in Britain. Though scholars like Owen and Sassoon skilled in writing iambic verse would transfer their experiences into poems as they served on the battlefields of Northern France. In 1914 mass production and sophisticated weaponry required workers and soldiers to have at least a basic education that had been denied most of them before the outbreak of war. For many British soldiers their uniforms were the first new set of clothes they had ever owned. This transition into the technological age makes the poetry of that period even more poignant. The trench poets comprising mainly of the officer class drew from their classical training to describe the situation of modern warfare where mankind was pitted against machines. In some ways one can draw a similar analogy with the modern Neil Young. In his mountain man clothes and boots creating a homely atmosphere at his concerts equipped with a Banjo or acoustic guitar. Against an audience backdrop of Mobil Phones and IPod's In many countries he faces an audience whose lives are crowded with what I would call the synthetic stress of virtual reality brought to them with the compliments of modern technology. When we hear his music or read his poetry we are sometimes transported to a place where we can get in touch with some of our basics emotions.

In the sixties there was a race to try and make priorities on what should be done first and what was important. Socially as a society the many restrictions and boundaries were removed and new ones set in place. As humans we developed a mindset that was formed by technological progress that was equaled by a spectacular creative process in which the two Neil's: 'Young and Armstrong' played a vital role that reflects the nature of humans to follow their instincts and improvise. Neil Young when he creates that subliminal wall of sound with the amps turned right up and the volume knobs on 'Old Black'[17] controlling the volume, you do not find that in any text books and Neil Armstrong who turned off the automatic computer steering when he saw the rough terrain and made the landing on the moon manually. They both had mentors, Young had Jimi Hendrix who radically changed the sound of the electric guitar and Armstrong had Chuck Yeager who was going to break the sound barrier no matter what.[18] The people who were part of the counter culture during the sixties were hip and the people who were not in tune with what was going on were known as square or straights. During the sixties there was a distinctive difference between these two types but now as we have gone into another millennium these once two very distinctive images have begun to merge. One way is through their children's marriages as seen in the film 'Meet the Fokker's' and the internet has given many people an outlet to be nonconformist. Vietnam vets are appreciated more today as part of a common guilt rather than being isolated and held as personally responsible for what could be called with hindsight a political error of judgment. Most people today appreciate the Beatles contribution to Western Culture even if they did not approve of them back then.

When researching anything with the word 'popular' attached to it in academic circles one is sometimes met with certain distance because it is not considered 'High Art.' The Beatles MA in Liverpool has the possibility to help trigger a change in attitude in academia concerning popular music. To quote Mike Brocken when asked about the different levels of art: "to me there is no high art or low art, it's just art".[19] This is very important because modern popular musicians and artists have become representatives of their followers and in many ways are comparable to statesmen in previous eras. John Lennon got his fingers burnt when he revealed to the media the importance of the Beatles to young people at that time making a comparison to the almighty. This was misinterpreted and had disastrous repercussions. He was right in pointing out the important position entertainers had in young people's lives at that time but wrong to draw religious parallels.

My research showed clearly how Neil Young closely interacted with the Civil Rights movement through his music. President Obama being sworn in as the first African American president of the United States of America can be seen as a direct consequence of the civil rights struggle in the 50's and 60's. The courage and actions of individual citizens like Dora Parks and sports celebrities like Mohammed Ali combined with the foresight and leadership of people like Martin Luther King were critical in laying the foundations to the quality of life that we have today. These people and this period deserve continuing recognition for its contribution.

For the Native American sources I have mainly looked at modern books written by Native Americans about their personal experiences growing up in the sixties and books based on memoirs from the last part of the 19th century which is the period Neil Young and Buffalo Springfield draw on for their stage image. I have tried to look at what was around in the North American that contributed to the post war environment that Neil Young and other country rock performers grew up in. I have described events and trends that might have influenced them in their formative years. There was an emphasis on Westerns in the entertainment industry during that period that influenced a whole generation. The evolution of the Beats also cumulated at the same time as the British invasion of America in the mid-sixties. These events build up to the time when the Buffalo Springfield was formed and is crucial to set the scene and help envision the situation that these two 19 year old guys; Neil Young and Stephen Stills, formed their band in.

Coincidently the last survivors of the First World War 1914-18 died in

2009 while I was doing my research. What have they got to do with a book about the sixties and Neil Young? You may ask, well with the death of these last three veterans in 2009. The Great War for civilization has passed from living memory. Like many of his generation J.R.R.Tolkien fought in that war and wrote "The Lord of the Rings" in memory of his friends who died so their sacrifice would not be forgotten. We all know LOTR but few of us knew his inspiration for writing the original story. Some of the battle scenes from the fields of Flanders are re-enacted in the battle for Middle Earth. That is one reason, another is that if veterans of Woodstock celebrated the occasion every year eventually there would be fewer of them. The ranks of the artists who played there have already begun to thin. I do not propose to measure the two events against each other or assume that the millions who died in the conflict that defined the beginning of the 20th century could be compared to the changes that occurred in the middle of that century. But as a historian I find both periods immensely fascinating and inspirational. The hopes and dreams of a time are sometimes built on something that calls for a sacrifice. The 20th century had many facets of this; the beginning, middle and end of each of these periods is marked by mass upheavals that deserve our attention if we are to acquire some form of understanding it. For the sixties we still have the films and music. One of the astonishing things about WW1 is even though it started almost 100 years ago it is still very accessible through second hand shops and eBay we can get memorabilia and letters. But like WW1 the sixties will also pass from living memory and that is why it is so important to focus on it now. The association I make is that both events were catalysts for the changes that occurred in the society afterwards. For example when I was a child many families had a living relative who served in WW1 and you often heard recollections. There was usually a piece of trench art on the mantel piece or a sepia print of a uniformed figure. In the same vein many young people have relatives who were active in the sixties either in civil rights or in choosing a radically different way of life to the one their parents had. They might read this book and say to their children "It wasn't like that where I grew up. Where I lived it happened like this." Through this process history becomes richer and the younger generation inherits a part of it by having a personal relationship to it. Old phonograph records known as LP's have almost passed on into the world of artifacts but LP covers can still decorate a space on the wall in a family home and at the same time not seem out of place as a museum exhibit. They are in a transitory period at the moment where they are not quite obsolete, thanks in part to diehards who claim that you can only get pure sound from vinyl.

I have tried to create a familiarity with the past and especially in connection with Neil Young by recollections of people who saw him at that time and by describing some of the events that shaped the time and some of the things that might have influenced his childhood and early career. To give an impression of the mood of that time I have used letters and recollections of 'Rusties' (Neil Young fans) who attended his concerts. Their snapshots of life back then and of the event and what it meant to them in their lives are extremely important to our understanding of Neil Young. What he means to them and what he meant to the period. Neil Young has created some impressive music during his long career and has accumulated a large group of followers of all ages from all over the world. I have tried to document what I found and hopefully anybody interested in that period in history will enjoy reading this book. I might not have come up with the right answers, but if I have activated some of your own thoughts and reflections about the period you will hopefully be able to make some of the connections between them and the things I have mentioned.

3. On the Road

Going on the road was a euphemism for many people in the sixties who left the security of their homes and jobs to look for something else in their lives. Some returned home after a short sojourn and for some it became habit forming where they returned home for intervals to earn money then left again. Some like Neil Young and Dylan never looked back. The original term probably came from "On the Road" a book by Jack Kerouac written in 1951 and when it was released in 1957 it was heralded as a revelation by the beat generation.

This book inspired many young people who read it to go on the road. The 16-year-old Barry Melton, who later became the lead guitarist of Country Joe and the Fish, read it in hospital. He then dropped out of college, and went on the road with his guitar.[20] Barry stated later that:

"I was happy for what I experienced in the sixties but I would not like to see them come back". [21]

On the Road seems to encapsulate the feeling of restlessness and frustration that some of the post war generation and large numbers of the sixties generation were able to relate to.

Ken Kesey said of the book in 1964 before he took his Merry Pranksters to New York in a psychedelic bus:

"We weren't old enough to be beatniks and we were a little too old to be hippies. But everyone I knew had read 'On the Road' and it opened up the doors to us just the way drugs did".[22]

In the book the main characters go on a road trip through the States and Mexico consuming beer, tequila and illicit substances. Various aspects of the book show the negative side of dropping out and going "on the road"; they shirk their responsibilities by leaving their young families behind. A similar situation appears in the musical "Hair" from 1968[23] where one of the leading actors Lafayette dressed in a tasselled, Native American style jacket abandons his young wife and child to follow the Hippie lifestyle.

Alex Forman worked with the Diggers[24] in a "Free Store" where you just took what you needed and if you had anything extra you did not need, you donated it. Alex saw the illusion of the hippie ethos they wanted to share with each other so people just took what they needed. The reality was some people were so poor they just took big boxes of stuff away to sell because they needed the money.

"There was abundance at a certain time for certain people. In early 1967, people would just give things away. On every street corner, there

would be somebody giving things away, free food, a free place to stay. Then in the summer of '67 was the Summer of Love. People started storming in thousands and within three months, there were people begging, 'Do you have free food?' In other words, so many people came that the surplus changed to scarcity. It got very ugly very fast. People got into really bad drugs like speed and heroin. There were rip-offs, violence, guns being drawn, people really malnourished, hepatitis, and people living in the street with no place to stay"[25]

This was one of the downsides of going on the road. It was not always a positive experience. Alex's statement encapsulates the situation perfectly. Something that started so idealistically did not really have much chance of surviving in a materialistic society. This was partially due to the mass influx of people who wanted to be a part of it. Some of them were sincere and some of them were just exploiting the situation. *"The Hippie died in 1968 not that good things from it don't remain because they most certainly do, but the cohesiveness and impetus faded"*. [26]

The situation for the 'Beats' was vastly different. To begin with they were mainly an elite group of middle class well educated intellectual guys who dropped in and out of the mainstream as it suited them or lived on royalties from their poetry and books. They were a privileged select group who basically did what they pleased, in the case of Gary Snyder he could easily adapt but not everyone finds the idea of living rough like a hobo or working as an 'oil wipe' on a ship attractive. The Beats could stay on the periphery of society because they were a minority group. Gary Snyder could not return to his State job as a fire lookout because he had been a member of what was seen as the socialistic seamen's union. For a Beat like him that was not a problem, he could just find something else like rip rapping. Whatever his job was it appeared to be secondary to his writing and lifestyle. Many 'Hippies' had a similar ethos; they worked all winter in a monotonous factory jobs then took the summer off. Many Americans headed to Europe for a six month sojourn.[27]

People in Europe headed for countries like Morocco, India or Kathmandu where the lifestyle seemed less synthetic and the drugs were abundant. Living in this way was only possible because of the good economic climate in the 50's and 60's. In a depression like the one in the 30's people had to live transitory lives, uprooted out of necessity, and many did not survive. The Counter culture and Hippy movements were basically youth orientated movements. This could be one of the reasons that 'Flower Power' eventually died out. As the capitalistic commercial elements in the society began to appreciate that youth culture was the new consumer mainstream alongside civil rights movements they affected and involved everybody. People's parents went out on strike for better conditions and wages and some marched in civil rights marches to obtain equality and equal rights. Many of the women's rights and equal rights movements that existed in the sixties continue to be represented by trade unions and other organizations today.

The military draft in the US meant a collective involvement of all families. Their children could now be called up; it was no longer a volunteer army. The war in South East Asia became increasingly unpopular as young people were forced to go. Another factor was, experience had shown that rebelling youths could be contained in the military and pressured to conform, Elvis being a case in point. Jerry Lee Lewis knew Elvis from the early Sun Record years, stated that the army had changed Elvis. Mohammed Ali then aptly named 'The Greatest' was not prepared to go down that road. As the heavy weight champion of the world he was a celebrity who spoke out more and more about social injustice especially against African Americans. He showed real mettle by refusing to go to a "war where white men were sending black men to kill yellow men". He said in a televised interview "no Cong ever called me Nigger". He gave many people strength and inspiration through his actions. He refused to go despite being threatened with prison and hounded by the media he was eventually stripped of his heavyweight world title and banned from boxing for five years. We stand humbled by this great man; this modern day Titan who became such an inspiration to so many people. After the ban he immediately reclaimed his title. Because of his status as world champion Mohamed Ali reached the masses all over the world. Most leaders or advocates of civil rights groups were mainly addressing their respective groups and a few others who had some sort of interest in the subject. Whereas Mohamed Ali was addressing the world through the press after he won his champion fight and people who expected to hear some mundane comments about how great the fight was were suddenly experiencing a political standpoint about the injustices to African Americans and the immorality of waging war. Other African American athletes like Tommie Smith and John Carlos followed suit in 1968 at the Olympics in Mexico by giving Black Power salutes during the medal ceremonies.[28]

Many of the civil rights movements achieved their aims with support from the counter culture. The benefits of these changes can still be seen in our societies today. Some of the sixties generation continue to carry with them ideals from the Hippie era. Charity organizations continue to prosper today even in a bad economic climate. The environment is a major issue for world governments. NGO's are a major political factor. More people including Neil Young now eat eco-friendly biological products.[29] Many of these things evolved as spin offs from the ideas that started during the Hippie era. People had to get back into the mainstream and earn a livelihood but because they had lived through the sixties, they knew life could be different. They are now among the most vigilant political consumers. It is important to point out that things that came out of that Hippie era have improved the quality of life today. One aspect is people have become more orientated on fulfilling their human potential in life rather than the pursuit of wealth. Men and women no longer have to stay locked in relationships they find unfulfilling. People have much more influence today in their jobs and the community they live in, through organizations and various committees. This shows the effects the sixties had on people and some of the lasting elements of the Beat and Hippy culture.

4. Gary Snyder and the Beats

Events in history rarely happen as spontaneous occurrences. There is always a buildup or process of events that led up to the change or a factor that triggers an event. Small things grow and small changes in the system can ultimately lead to larger significant changes. For example, a petition for the abolition of slavery inspires someone to start a movement that can lobby government and help achieve that aim. The inspiration for the petition in the first place must have come from an idea, an act, or experience. In the same process the beat poets and beatniks were influential to the sixties counter culture movement. Graham Nash says he was inspired by the Beat poets to write Marrakech Express.[30] One of the poets Gary Snyder had a strong commitment to the natural environment and he promoted the Native American religion and lifestyles in the 1960´s as a viable alternative to mainstream materialistically motivated capitalistic lifestyle that dominated in the US. People at that time were looking at alternative faiths, Eastern religions and different forms of meditation. Snyder tried to make people aware that with the Native American culture, America already had an indigenous religion based on a closer relationship to nature. Gary Snyder received a Pulitzer Prize for his collection of Poems "Turtle Island" in 1977. Snyder never became the household name that Ginsberg was on an international level. Ginsberg was one of the Beats figureheads he associated with Bob Dylan and had hosted the first "Happening" in the UK called "The First Communion." at the Royal Albert Hall. An event that was experienced by even more people as it was made into a film by the director Peter Whitehead as a way of documenting the sixties lifestyle. The evolution of the Beats during the 1950´s was an important part of what happened in the sixties. The original Beats were a decidedly American phenomena supported by a Californian climate, the UK has only one climate zone; cold, grey and drizzle. Snyder got some of his inspiration from working with Native Americans at logging camps and Rip Rapping. During his 10 year sojourn living as a Buddhist Monk in Japan he experienced how in the Asia old religions survived and were practiced side by side with the new religions. Contrary to practice In the Western World where religions became officially obsolete when they were replaced by new ones. Snyder recognized that the planet played a key role as the mother in the Native American religions. These religions incorporated the different aspects of nature into its vision of life. Before he went to Asia, Snyder got inspiration from living and working in the nature as a fire guard and lumberjack. When he returned, he tried to promote in his writings the virtues of the Native American and their relationship to nature. Kerouac was a creative writer and definitely did not subscribe to the Hippie ethos. Snyder saw himself as a Buddhist and did not like to be categorized as a Beat. He preferred to see himself and a Californian renaissance poet who promoted the re-emergence of Native American values that had existed in the US long before colonization. Despite this he is closely associated with the Beats and their work: he was the inspiration for Jack Kerouac's character 'Jack Cassidy' in the book Dharma Bums which became one of the counter cultures bibles. He helped Ginsberg organize the gathering of the tribes and gave a poetry reading there. They promoted another set of values by handing out psychedelic drugs that radically changed young people's perceptions about life. At the time of the Gathering of the Tribes, young people were drastically increasing their consumption of these types of drugs.

Although Neil Young never mentions the Beats, Gary Snyder was a very popular poet figure during the 'Summer of Love.' He was living and working in the same location as Neil Young and the Buffalo Springfield. It would be hard to imagine that Neil Young never came across his work. We know that he followed what Bob Dylan was doing. Dylan and Ginsberg were close friends and often photographed together in publicity shots. "Rolling Stone Magazine" was the top counter culture music magazine at time. Neil Young was interviewed by Rolling Stone during the sixties and seventies and he would have read reviews about major events like Woodstock.[31] This magazine covered big events and highlighted the direct association between the Beats and the Native Americans as they organized events in San Francisco called "Happenings" like the famous Gathering of the Tribes in 1967. Native

American styles were used by the Hippies in the San Francisco Bay area. With all this happening: posters, advertisements and Hippies wearing Native American clothes in California and San Francisco where Neil Young and the Buffalo Springfield were playing he could not have avoided noticing what was going on. As explained by Deloria, during this period young Americans became more conscious of their heritage and the historical roots that connected them to the indigenous peoples of America. This awareness could have influenced Neil Young in his choice of wearing Native American regalia. As a young man growing up Gary Snyder was surrounded by nature. Going for trips in the mountains and absorbing the sheer power of the American wilderness. Neil Young uses the same imagery in his work. Snyder worked for logging companies that had many Native American employees he made notes of his experiences and the stories that he heard. One of Neil Young's most popular images is that of the 'Mountain Man' when he wears logging shirts and jeans and light tan boots with a short suede jacket. This is the type of clothing used by loggers during the 1950's and later. Like Cowboys, Loggers are representative of the outdoor life working in the nature with an element of danger.

After his Asian odyssey Snyder returned to the states in the mid-sixties. At this time the counterculture was gathering momentum. By the time the Gathering of the Tribes took place he could see how American had become spiritually and culturally poorer. As a solution, he advocates adopting aspects of the Native American culture which is indigenous to America. Snyder had experienced in the Buddhist teachings that people followed many different gods. It was a reversal of what the European settlers did when they came to America and suppressed the religions and rituals of the Native Americans and tried to convert them to Christianity. Snyder saw much of the beauty and values of Native American way of life and their relationship with nature. He incorporated this in his work in San Francisco at that time. The whole counter culture movement acknowledges the role of the Beats as wise men or founding fathers who showed the way to a new perception of how to live life.

5. The Sixties Generation

The Beat poets became the role models for large segments of the counter culture, among them musicians and hippies started to follow the bohemian lifestyle epitomized by the Beatniks. This group supplied an alternative to the 'Little Boxes'[32] theory that Pete Seeger sang about in 1963 in this song he described the conventional career path as following a pre calculated route through life and living in "little boxes that all looked just the same "and basically doing what everybody else was doing or had already done. After hearing the song, a professor at the University of Miami said: "I've been lecturing my classes about middleclass conformity for a whole semester. Here's a song that says it all in 1½ minutes."[33] The music and lyrics during the sixties from people like Dylan and the Beatles gave many people a crash course in the University of Life. For many young people working regular jobs it was their only source of education on how to escape the hum drum of their daily existence. After taking these crash courses by smoking joints and listening to music many young people started to break away from these tried and tested pathways and follow alternative routes. They embraced the opportunities that they encountered or they returned to the tried and tested pathways. The Beats wrote poetry and books that became an inspiration and guide to young people in the sixties. The pillars of established American culture were falling and being replaced by totem poles. Allan Ginsberg who realized this published the poem "Howl" in 1955.[34] The Harvard professor Timothy Leary of "Turn on, Tune in and Drop out" fame and later dismissed from the university for his research on LSD in 1963.[35] Leary and others were leading the way for the counter culture revolution that would eventually help to form the conscience of a generation. It was not just the music and artistic expression that dominated. People's attitude to everything started to change. They viewed war, race and government policies far more critically than ever before. In the early years of the 20th century youth was bought up to specifically serve the society. The British and French dominated the world with their empires and their citizens aspired to serve it. After the allied suppression of Germany at the end of WW1, America and

President Wilson had a 14 point proposal that would have changed the world and possibly led to a more harmonious Europe. But England and France rejected the 14 points and chose to continue suppressing Germany and claiming war retributions that would eventually cripple her. This scheme collapsed when Germany went bankrupt during the economic crisis of the Great Depression. During the early 1930's, Germany and Japan started to educate and indoctrinate the young generation into fascists whose blood would be shed around the globe in WW2. At the end of WW2 there was a drastic shift in the balance of power. America became the accepted world leader, France and the UK were deregulated and Europe was forced to work together much as Wilson had planned 27 years earlier.

The young people of the free world were encouraged to adopt the American culture and ways through products and TV shows. The American lifestyle held an infatuation that was without precedence leading the way musically with Jazz, Blues and finally Rock and Roll. To the young people things American seemed to be without the confinements that were associated with the European way of life. For example eating something and walking around or talking with your mouth full was considered bad manners in the UK, now with the advent of bubble gum you were chewing all the time and blowing bubbles in between sentences. Some of it could have been due to the fact that as a country America was less than 200 years old and it was not restricted by a ridged class system and ancient traditions. It appeared to have a more accessible education system as shown by the GI bill after WW2. The Beats also evolved in this system and somehow found freedom to develop their philosophy and alternative lifestyle. They promoted the idea that people could change their lives if they wanted, collectively or individually. Their view was that there was a place for the parallel society and alternative culture inside the present society if some of the rules were changed to accommodate it. This seemed to be the main goal at the time and one can say with hindsight that it did not succeed but some of the rules were changed and remained changed. The counter culture eventually learned to co-exist in a society abiding by rules that had become more open minded and allowed more equality for women and ethnic minority groups like the African Americans. Things like national conscription (the draft) to fight a war and attitudes about sexual orientation were questioned. The early obscenity court cases in the UK like the one against D.H. Lawrence's book "Fanny Hill" showed how wide the gap was between the ruling classes and the populace when the judge said:

"Would want your family or even your servants to read this book".

The ruling classes did indeed have servants at that time. In 1960 only about 2 % of school leavers attended university this changed radically during the sixties not only due to changes in the class structure but the demand from industry for more qualified workers. Into these winds of change blowing through Britain the beats organized the first 'Be Ins' in London modeled on the Californian "Gathering of the Tribes". The definition "Gathering of the Tribes" is very well chosen as it describes the different tribes coming together based on the ancient Native American tradition. By bringing people together these actions spread the ideas of the counter culture around the world. There is no doubt that the Beats played a major role in the influencing what became the counter culture by laying down some guidelines and showing through their own experience that it was possible to follow an alternative lifestyle. This lifestyle preceded the counter culture and the Beats became role models for the sixties generation.

Artistically with "Howl" Ginsberg had rejected the conventional world of poetry and poets like Gary Snyder had been on the road (or on the sea) searching for some deeper meaning even to the extent of practicing Asian religions. After achieving this knowledge he returned like in a 'hero saga' to share the knowledge with his people. Gary Snyder lived as a monk in Japan and when he returned to the States he wrote with empathy and compassion about the life of the Native American and simple chores of homesteading like the poem axe handles. He illustrates that these simple acts have a spiritual meanings and that the rhythm of physical work contributes to the rhythm of poetry.

The Beatles acknowledge that they were influenced by the Beats in the very early days. During the sixties there was a convergence of many of the points I have mentioned. There was a fusion as they became entwined and interacted with each other. Without a doubt the expansion of the Cultural Revolution that took place during the sixties was facilitated in part[36] by the economic prosperity in the Western World at that time. Without this surplus of money things would certainly not have happened on the scale they did.

The Labour Government in the UK under Prime Minister Harold Wilson has to take some credit for the developments. Labour saw that Britain could no longer be a major world power alongside the USA and USSR so they focused on changing the society internally starting the open university and generously funding many Art colleges where many of the budding rock artists from modest backgrounds like Lennon, Clapton, Townshend and Bowie and fashion designers like Mary Quant served their apprentices under teachers like Peter Blake. The harvest of these creative seeds was that Swinging London became an international fashion and music capitol that to a large extent dictated the styles and direction worldwide.

People flocked to London where it was happening on this side of the Atlantic. The British element was further reinforced by pop music bands touring the world conquering the world market. In the vanguard was the British invasion of America spearheaded by the Beatles who opened up the American market for other British bands like the Rolling Stones, Hollies and the Who. This world market gave an unprecedented economic boost to Britain and whether or not that had been Labours intention is debatable. However what is not debatable is that the quality of life improved vastly in Britain for the working classes who were the poorest in Europe. Unlike Germany and France and other European countries workers in the UK did not have the advantage of workers committees sitting in on board meetings. On the continent in what is now known as the EU, workers were protected by laws concerning minimum wages and working hours.

Ironically the conditions and quality of life of the German workers were far superior to those of their English counterparts

In America it was the civil rights movement and the War in Vietnam that occupied a big part of people's consciousness and played a major part in people's attitudes to the counter culture. Consequently these events influenced world opinion concerning American politics. Many of the progressive radical elements in the music and film industry started to interact with events of the time. I use an example given by Helicopter pilots in Vietnam flying back from missions against a backdrop of Crosby Stills Nash and Young music, they said; "We heard the anthems of our generation". Neil Young wrote the song 'Ohio' about the four students who were shot dead protesting against the bombing of Cambodia which they saw as an escalation of the conflict in Vietnam. The song gave young people a sense of unity and helped unite them. This song and the single "War Song" which he recorded with Graham Nash showed Neil Young's opposition to the war in South East Asia. The draft in America brought the young people together because it affected everybody. It was because they had been forced into the situation that young de-mobbed GI's could grow their hair long and still wear their military M1 field jackets and not be ostracized by their peers. The Beatles, Jimi Hendrix, Eric Clapton and many others in the counter culture favoured military jackets because they had a connection to them through their class and culture.

In the film industry movies like Little Big man and Soldier Blue had an effect on the attitude people had of the war. The films not only showed parallels with the way the American military was acting in Vietnam but also gave a more realistic view of its past conduct toward Native Americans. The injustices against Native Americans had been covered up by historical inaccuracies for decades and during the sixties many of these historical events were taken up for revision. A good example of this is given by Vine Deloria, Jr. the Native American author who wrote the Indian Manifesto Custer Died for your Sins. In his description of the aftermath of what was then called The Battle of Wounded Knee:

"The War Department always insisted that it had been a 'battle' to stamp out the Ghost Dance religion among the Sioux. This does not however, explain bayoneted Indian women and children found miles from the scene of the incident." [37]

Deloria clearly illustrates the misrepresentation of historical events. When a highly trained Calvary unit of professional soldiers gets killed it is referred to as "Custer's Massacre." When they attack an Indian village of mainly women and children it is called a 'Battle'. Vine Deloria's quote clearly shows the image whites had of Native Americans before the revision. It was the combined efforts during the sixties of many different organizations, individuals, film makers, writers and musical artists that helped to change this image. Alongside the civil rights movement the counter culture emerged and spread throughout the Western world. One of the major dimensions of the counter culture was the explosion of music and creativity that symbolized the era. This shows how many things were interacting at the time Buffalo Springfield was formed there were chain reactions to external and internal events. One of the external elements was the invasion of America by British pop groups. The result of this was that bands started to dominate the US music charts that had previously been the dominated by solo artists. It also provoked an upsurge in American bands inspired by the Beatles.

In 1964 the Beatles were playing a concert in Paris when they heard that "I Want to Hold Your Hand" had reached number one in America. They were in awe of the US as the home of Rock and Roll and reaching number one there was a crowning achievement. The single was the first Beatles single to be recorded on a four track recorder. In America the single was released on the album "Meet the Beatles" the LP actually outsold the single (something that had never happened before). In the same year 1964 the Stones topped the UK charts with a Chicago blues number "Little Red Rooster" an achievement which Keith Richards was justifiably proud of because the UK pop charts had never had a blues number one; ironically it was banned in the US because of the sexual overtones.[38] The Beatles opened up America for other British bands to go over and perform their music and in the process make some money. This in turn gave American bands that had previously been in a market dominated by solo acts a chance to get support from American record companies to counter balance the British invasion. An internal element was a resurgence of interest in American history from the late 19th century. In the States during the 1950's Country and Western ballads were popular and children grew up on John Ford Westerns along with TV shows that had Western themes. This identification by Americans with the "Wild West" at that time can be seen as evidence that many people saw the men of that era who closed the frontier as the real founding fathers of America who carved an existence out of the wilderness unburdened by religious ideology. When the new Country Rock look was created it coincided with the arrival of Spaghetti Westerns made in Spain and Italy and a new wave of home-grown westerns. The "Counterculture Westerns" in 1964-65 films like Cheyenne Autumn "these films suggested that Native American culture might be a morally superior alternative to civilization" These films appeared just as American critics and scholars were undertaking a broad and thoroughgoing re-evaluation of Native American history and ethnography" [39]

Films like Ford's were a good thing for awareness in academic circles but they were not popular in the mainstream. The ones that made a significant impact on the American market were the 'Spaghetti Westerns.'[40] These Westerns were very much in the spirit of the times. With modern music and bright colours in the credits, they had much in common with the popular James Bond films of the period. Sergio Leone's directing style of ultra-close ups. The character of Clint Eastwood, the epitome of the 'anti-hero', appealed to audiences of the time (and re-launched Lee Van Cleef's career). Eastwood smoked small cigars and was clad in a poncho and jeans. Some of the cast wore tasselled buckskin jackets. The poncho Eastwood wore was very much like the one worn by Stephen Stills at Woodstock. Together on stage with a heavy mustached David Crosby in his tasselled jacket a look that was credited inspiration for Billy, Captain America's side kick in the film

Easy Rider. The new look of authenticity in Westerns was more rough and ready, the characters were now unwashed and unshaven. Native Americans actors were used to portray Native Americans instead of European Americans in makeup. There was a craving at the time for authenticity and it shows how the music and film industry seemed to converge and complement each other. Just listen to John Hammond's raw acoustic soundtrack to 'Little Big Man' compared to an orchestrated soundtrack of a John Ford Western. At the same time research was going on at another level to re-evaluate the history of the Native American. If incidents like "Sand Creek" and "Wounded Knee" could be portrayed realistically in movies as they were in Little Big Man they could have an influence on the mainstream that in turn put pressure on the policy makers. They could also be interpreted as analogies to what was happening in Vietnam and in that way they gave support to the antiwar movement.

This all became part of a cultural seismic process that started to change life for everyone. A major influence on what was happening at the time was the Cold War which provoked the Vietnam War , the ideology was 'no more ground could be given to the communists. They must not be able to increase their sphere of influence in the world. They were seen as a threat to our way of life.' The civil rights movement and the explosion of 'Youth Culture' created the anti-war movement and crossed over and influenced the music and film industries in what music was produced and in what type of films were made. This crossover effect sometimes resulted in phenomenal artistic and economic success for the industry and the artists. Music in films has always had recognition usually in the form of a theme tune that gets an Oscar nomination thereby becoming popular and reaching a larger audience. The success of the music from some of the counter culture movies in terms of LP sales really reflected the immense influence the movement had on young people worldwide. Millions of people around the world saw the film Woodstock when it was released in 1970. At that time this musical documentary gave movie theatre audiences a feeling of community similar to the one felt by the people at the event.

Another musical mover and shaker released just before Woodstock was the road movie Easy Rider (1969): A low budget film that cost a half a million of non-studio dollars and grossed 19 million dollars. Hollywood suddenly realised the buying power of young people and the existence of a large market for socially relevant movies. The story of Easy Rider was symbolic of the closing of the decade where "Captain American" and "Billy" go on a road trip through America. Captain America wore a Stars and Stripes helmet and leather jacket while his sidekick Billy was clad in a Native American style Buckskin tasselled jacket with a cowboy hat and his long hair and moustache looking very much like David Crosby (of Crosby Stills &Nash). The audience identified with the films message and loved the phenomenal Rock soundtrack which featured among others: Hendrix, Steppenwolf and the Byrds.[41] This is a perfect example of how the conjuncture of external elements combined to influence other events when they converged at a certain time in History.

If you focus on the 1960's this was a period in American history where many events occurred at the same time. This period can be seen as a testing time and coming of age for the United States and its post WW2 role as world leader. Fortunately due to the social revolution taking place at the time it was not just a build-up in military strength as seen in the Soviet Union but a period of laying new ground rules concerning how people would live in Western Society based largely on the expectations of the young generation. How did it all lead up to this? Well for start major events from the last century like the closing of the frontier were still within living memory. Plus TV shows and films using themes from that period were influencing the generation growing up. Veterans from WW1 and WW2 were still visible in the society. The Korean War where massive Chinese participation had prevented an American victory had been over for only seven years. There is a Cold War with Russia and a hot war in Vietnam where fear of Chinese involvement as in Korea limits American possibilities of victory. Many WW2 veterans were now parents to teenagers who burned draft cards and became involved in the antiwar movement. America is in a Space Race against the Soviet Union trying to get to the moon. The economic growth during sixties in the United States and Europe is unprecedented and has become known as ¨The Golden Age.¨ These are the external factors that policy makers grew up with. The older they were the more factors they could identify with. When the director John Ford was a child bandits were still in existence in isolated areas and he personally knew the US Marshall Wyatt Earp who was a historical icon. This identification with the Wild West and the use of force as a solution was deeply engraved in the American psyche. Settlers had used force to take America from its indigenous peoples and afterwards founded a country based on freedom and equality. The paradox being of course that this freedom and equality was only for the chosen few with the right credentials. Internally within American society something [42] else started to evolve because of various cultural developments. Under the leadership of Martin Luther King very large numbers of African Americans were starting to demand their civil rights. This resulted in many violent demonstrations and confrontations between African Americans and the authorities. This was the final battle against injustice that a civil war had been fought for one hundred years previously. The demands were simple 'equality and an end to segregation throughout the USA'.

Parallel to what was happening in the civil rights movement young people from all backgrounds started dropping out in significant numbers, shunning education and careers and refusing to be drafted to Vietnam. It started with isolated incidents but soon gained momentum and evolved into a major movement, where universities closed and young demonstrators clashed with police and national guardsmen. Around the same time a counter culture greatly inspired by the Beats of the previous decade sprung up. These young people start to find role models among the sixties musicians whose music was inspired by the black music of the previous decade: Rhythm & Blues, Rock and Roll.[43] With the advent of cheap transistor radios Rock and Roll music was heard everywhere, suddenly there was a soundtrack to accompany young people through the mundane routines of daily life. The various groups interacted during that period. The Country Rock music evolved in that period and Neil Young's visual image in Comanche war shirt with bear claw necklace vastly contributed to a broader understanding of Native American culture and in that way helped them in their struggle for civil rights by making it among other things 'cool to be an Indian.' All these segments of different things that were happening in the sixties influenced and interacted with each other. In the final analysis this contributed to various relevant changes in the society like the end of segregated restaurants and schools in the South. Native Americans got more control and self-determination over the way they lived their lives. Furthermore it is clear that the many different forces were starting to have an effect on the values of Western society and influence other aspects for example censorship in the entertainment industry. In the UK with films like 'A taste of Honey' contained three themes that were considered taboo at the time; interracial relationships, single mothers and homosexuality (which was still illegal in the UK at that time.) Another TV film 'Cathy Come Home' highlighted unemployment and homelessness among young couples, both these films contributed immensely to radical changes in the law and censorship.

6. The British Invasion

In 1963 Beatlemania took Great Britain by storm. The world was changing rapidly due to the economic boom. People in the UK now had more leisure time. For the first time since the war some workers found they even had some excess money. Rationing started in Great Britain in January 1940 and ended 14 years later in July 1954. Up to then people had mainly bought things out of necessity now there was money to buy some things simply for pleasure. Even parents who did not like the 'Fab Four' or 'Mop Tops' had to begrudgingly admit that they were skilled craftsmen playing their instruments and singing their own songs. Under the management of Brian Epstein they went from strength to strength. Epstein ran the family music and record shop in Liverpool within walking distance of the 'Cavern Club' where the Beatles played. After punters repeatedly came in asking for an obscure record by Tony Sheridan and the Beatles on the German Polydor label his curiosity was aroused.

Epstein had always imagined that the Beatles were a German band until a customer told him that they were in fact a local band that had just returned from Hamburg. Epstein walked down the street to see them play at one of their lunchtime gigs. What he saw in the crowded dark smoke filled cellar convinced him that these guys had the potential to be big. He did not foresee the massive reaction to their music but as he put it 'They had star quality, whatever that is, they had it'. Brian Epstein was a local boy from Liverpool which was one of Great Britain's major ports that had prospered during the 19th century during the heyday of the British Empire. In comparison life in the North in the early sixties was pretty bleak. The center of entertainment was London and the whiskey belt where the affluent middle classes lived was situated in the area South of London. The North was coal mines, steelworks and factories that had produced some football clubs and some comedians. Generally at that time there was no place in the South for people with regional dialects especially in the entertainment business.

Liverpool where the Beatles came from was a predominately a working class area, inhabited by people who manned the machines in factories, worked in the docks.

In Manchester where Graham Nash lived young men went down the mines or worked in factories. However working people had always had their own culture and throughout British history they had enjoyed social events like music hall and going down the pub for a sing song. This form of entertainment in clubs and pubs gave a lot of early bands their introduction to performing live and developing their skills. These venues had strict licensing laws and did not run all night like the Star Club in Hamburg where the Beatles really learnt their craft and evolved into one of the tightest bands around. Epstein contracted the Beatles and became their manager. The Mersey Sound developed and suddenly regional accents were all the rage. Epstein recruited more Northern acts and was constantly promoting his new finds. The Beatles became huge in the UK but the American record companies were not interested in groups at that time. Previous acts like Cliff Richard had not appealed to the North American market. There were some individuals like Neil Young who through connections in Winnipeg had early access to records by bands like The Shadows. These bands were so unknown at the time that Neil Young could play their songs at high school dances and pass them off as his own compositions! According to misguided PR managers of US record companies groups like the Beatles did not stand a chance, solo artists were what appealed to the young American audience. The first Beatle records released in the States came out on small obscure labels like 'Vee-jay.' A very important aspect of Beatlemania and the fans adoration of their music was that it was not artificially created by Epstein or the record industry. He was a business man who saw the possibilities in what was basically an 'attractively scruffy bunch' of musicians who had a great sound.

From the beginning Epstein declared the Beatles cared little about their appearance but were totally dedicated to their sound. It was through the sound that the fans made their first acquaintance with the Beatles music. This was also true in America when DJ's got hold of Beatle records from Europe and started playing them, the audience could not get enough. Epstein was sure the Beatles could break America and the British invasion came in three waves, the first one was a 14 day reconnaissance sortie in 1964 where Epstein was testing the waters. He had cunningly booked them on the Ed Sullivan show which gave them a wide audience. Apart from that he only booked them to play in medium size venues. Epstein was not sure of success and he did not want the adverse publicity of the Beatles playing to half empty halls.

Epstein knew all about image, he took the Beatles out of leather jackets and jeans and put them in collarless suits inspired by German design. He focused on their image and left the creative side of making music up to the band. Having recognized very early the vital role played by the media he never let the Beatles deplane until he could see all the press photographers were in place to record the Fab Four as they made their entrance waving to the crowds. The Ed Sullivan show Feb. 9th 1964 had a crowd of around 728, screaming fans.[44] The reaction was the same as it had been in England and Epstein quickly realized that the American fans did not need time to get acquainted with the Beatles. The British invasion had begun the biggest venues they played during this initial tour was Washington Coliseum February 8th with 8,092, screaming fans.[45] When they returned in August for the second wave most of the venues had double this capacity. In their wake would come a wave of British bands with an overrepresentation of the Mersey Sound many of them managed by Epstein. He managed the business end and the artists wrote and performed the music or Epstein borrowed from the Lennon and McCartney catalogue.

Most of these bands including the Beatles were untrained musicians. They were able to reproduce the sound they wanted through collaborating with sound engineers and producers like George Martin who was open and receptive to their ideas in the studio. Importantly in many cases these producers and technicians shared their knowledge with the fledging musicians who then went on to become accomplished record producers in their own right. This is a critical point, the first Buffalo Springfield album was very badly mixed and as Ritchie Furay later stated:

 "Who knows what we might have sounded like if we had George Martin in the studio".

There were distinctive parallels between the Buffalo Springfield and the Beatles both bands were devoted to their music, which was built around two exceptional singer songwriters. But the early Buffalo Springfield lacked good management and good record production along with PR. Brian Epstein was already on the periphery in British society due to his Jewish background and his homosexuality. He was not that much older than the Beatles so as a young man he could relate to their outlook in many ways. Acknowledging his contribution Paul McCartney said after Epstein died *"if anyone was the fifth Beatle, it was Brian."* In the early interviews his upper class accent clearly sets him apart from the scouse dialect of his wonder group. Epstein had wanted to be an actor and had attended RADA drama school in London alongside classmates 'Peter

O'Toole, Albert Finney and Susannah York.' Finney who turned down a CBE and a Knighthood saying they perpetuated snobbery, O'Toole who had eight Oscar nominations (three more than Finney) and was also reputed to have turned down a knighthood was also an anti-war activist. Susannah York was left wing politically and spoke out against Israel's nuclear program. This was an important time for Epstein because his period at RADA, where he mixed with these young radicals, whose exceptionally strong personalities must have made an impression on him. In much the same way they influenced their public through their actions during their careers.

After RADA Epstein went into the family music business whole heartedly and wrote a column in the local music paper on new releases. The fact that he had been trained at the Royal Academy of Dramatic Art gained him credibility with the Beatles and they respected his views on entertainment protocol. They followed [46]his directions about dress code and started wearing suits. He changed their image onstage when they performed. They were no longer allowed to end songs at random when they felt like it. They had to stop eating, drinking and smoking onstage and no more swearing. It was Epstein who suggested the synchronized bow that the Beatles used at the end of their performances. Altogether Epstein's influence made their visual presentation much more sophisticated and polished.

He passionately believed that the Beatles could be a major success and after being turned down by nearly every major record company in the UK his strength of conviction finally convinced George Martin to sign them to Parlophone an EMI subsidiary. Martin was a veteran of the Guildhall Music and Drama School in the early fifties. He had worked recording classical music and some light comedy acts like Peter Sellers and Spike Milligan of Goon show fame and Michael Flanders and Donald Swann who wrote the Tony Hancock scripts. His big breakthrough as a producer that made his company Parlophone profitable was recording the show 'Beyond the Fringe' a milestone in British satire that played in the West End and Broadway in the early sixties.

Having had success with some of these improbable projects must have influenced George Martin's judgment and given him a more open minded attitude when he met Epstein. All the other producers saw no prospect in the Beatles and turned him down. Another aspect was that Epstein and Martin had the same social status although originally Martin came from a different class background. They were both following relatively unorthodox careers when you consider their backgrounds. It was Epstein's enthusiasm and commitment to the success of the Beatles that helped convince Martin.

It is also possible that Epstein himself did not fully understand the Beatles attraction but he had worked in his record shop in Liverpool and seen the enthusiasm they created among young fans that kept coming in asking for that obscure German single by Tony Sheridan and the Silver Beatles. In the beginning George Martin did not find them particularly talented musicians but he liked their sense of humour. After the recording session Martin asked them if there was anything they personally did not like, to which George Harrison replied: *"Well there's your tie for a start"*. As Lennon and McCartney followed up Harrison's comment with jokes and comic wordplay Martin decided they were worth signing for their wit alone! Was this the 'Star Quality' Epstein talked about? Something that was hard to define but somehow recognizable when you encountered it?

George Martin said later EMI had not taken such a big risk and really had nothing to lose by signing on the Beatles because in the contract it stipulated that the Beatles would only get one penny in commission for every record sold and that was divided between the four of them! Epstein got the recording contract and telegraphed the boys who were playing in Hamburg that a recording date had been fixed June 6th 1962. With his business acumen and unconventional personal traits Epstein was not afraid to squeeze the lemon or push the envelope. The Beatles used to quip at him "How far are we gonna go Brian?" to which his standard reply was "All the way boys". This was not a collection of individuals who were afraid to rock the boat. Epstein was a man who at that time could have gone to prison for his sexual orientation and the battle hardened Beatles were certainly not intimidated by the press or prepared to conform and sit back and reap the benefits of their endeavours. The more fame and fortune they got the more they took control over their work and career. Their personal tastes and expressions started to manifest themselves in a way that would inspire a generation. Under a bronze statue of them in Liverpool stands *"Four lads who shook the world"* and with the help of Brian Epstein that is exactly what they did. Their apprenticeships and acquired experience came from playing pubs, clubs and dance halls in Britain and Germany that were rough and ready, fights often broke out and Lennon along with other contemporaries like Rodger Daltrey were notorious for getting into fights. The Beatles became a fixture at the Star Club which is situated in the Red Light District in Hamburg known as the Reper Bahn. Hamburg was West Germany's major seaport at that time[47] and it can be compared to Liverpool in many ways, except of course for a legal red light district and clubs that were not restricted by stringent opening hours. The Beatles have said in interviews that it was common for waiters to lace drinks with pep pills so bands played all night. The Stones encountered a similar relaxed attitude in Italy where amphetamine could be bought at the chemists over the counter. Opportunities like those in Hamburg did not exist in prudish England; clubs in London were very expensive and very exclusive.

By playing regularly at the Star Club these young guys were cutting their teeth in what was one of the most exciting places for night life in Europe. To illustrate just how young they were on their first trip there they were actually deported from Germany because George Harrison was too young to get a work permit. When fame came to them after seasoning experiences like these the Beatles would counter-attack the press with a vengeance! Lighting up their fags and giving loaded answers like Lennon's when accused of corrupting America's youth he fired back; *"we didn't create the music you did"*.[48] This self-confidence combined with a musical skill and stage presence gained from years of experience playing Rock and Roll made them an extremely tight band.

Just look at the news reel from Shea Stadium and the Hollywood Bowl. One of the best examples of the Beatles playing live is the 1967 performance in Tokyo on Japanese TV. Here they are all still wearing the German style collarless Beatle suits. The band is really tight and adjusts faulty mike stands in the middle of songs without missing a beat, this was live and not the 'playback' that was sometimes evident on the early 'Ready Steady Go' shows. The energy when they played their new single 'Paperback Writer' and showmanship as Lennon casually slides his thumb down the bass strings on a riff. They were a great live band no doubt about that. British bands like the Stones are in agreement that the Beatles opened the American market for them.

The Beatles played their own instruments skillfully and filled their LP's with masterfully written songs. They wrote so many songs they could give them away. One of them was 'I Wanna Be Your Man' which was covered by Ringo on their second album 'With the Beatles'. The story goes Lennon and McCartney met the Stones on the street and heard they needed material so they went into the studio with them and finished writing 'I Wanna Be Your Man'. It became the Stones first hit reaching number 12 in the UK chart.[49] For aspiring American bands like The Byrds and Buffalo Springfield the Beatles must have been an enormous inspiration.

The Byrds actually started as a band doing covers of Beatles songs in LA and the Buffalo Springfield name Revolver and Ringo on the cover of their second album as inspirations. This album opens with Neil Young's Mr. Soul where you hear the screaming fans in the intro; the screams are taken from a recording of the Beatles concert at the Cow Centre. This clip was probably chosen for the intensity more than admiration for the band. One of the Beatles crucial roles in music was in setting markers and showing bands what could be achieved. They made films and concept albums and long singles and became a dominant world force in the industry. Right from the start they refused to compromise where their art was concerned. To illustrate where peoples interests were at the time, more TV viewers around the world watched Elvis

Presley's Hawaii Concert than saw the moon landing. The Beatles showed anything was possible with the right selection of people and the right sequence of events. If Epstein saw the world was ready for the Beatles or not can be debated what cannot be debated is that the sound the Beatles created filled a niche in people's lives and all their tomfoolery and larking around on camera was readily embraced.

The world was their oyster and ripe for picking. But they had also earned the fruits of their endeavours. Along with the endless touring and driving up and down the country, doing live shows plus radio and TV. They were also incredibly lucky to be in that time and that place, when a world full of young people who were ready for a change. Their records reinforced by films like 'Help' that had almost Pythonesque comedy sequences.

In the UK this resulted in colour suddenly coming into young people's drab existence. It is very hard to visualize now how dull things really were at that time. When designer Mary Quant started, girls had a choice of two colours for their shoes, black and brown. When she introduced white boots and miniskirts many of the older generation were incensed and accused her of corrupting the youth and their morals. After the excitement of America where there was something was going on all the time the Beatles knew life could be different. When they returned Ringo was asked *"What do you like about America?"* he replied *"Everything, things move so much faster there and everything is going on at once, not to mention sunshine"*.

Neil Young must have had similar impressions in California after living in Canada. Back in the 1950's Canada was pretty provincial compared to the US and many Canadian musical artists like Leonard Cohen, Joni Mitchell and Buffy Saint Marie chose to reside in America. I do not maintain that the Beatles were responsible for the all the changes that came about at that time. There was an economic upswing and quality of life became better. Things were not just on a subsistence level as they had been for most working class people in the UK since the Second World War.

I believe many people who lived through that period would agree the Beatles laid down the soundtrack for the sixties that young people related to. As Paul Weller stated in a recent NME interview *"The Beatles were my musical heroes. You could always expect something more from them they were constantly pushing the boundary"* He was growing up in the provinces where you came home from school or work and put on a record to feel good and you went to the dance hall on Friday night.[50]

In the beginning the music did not transcend generations but on their final US tours older people were present in the audiences and many parents accompanying their besotted kids became converts to the sound. It was not just loud, fast Rock and Roll songs there were many ballads and slow love songs as well. Songs like 'Things we said today', 'And I love her', 'Yes it Is' and 'Yesterday'. These are beautiful articulate love songs that inspired many groups and singers like Paul Simon to sing ballads accompanying himself on acoustic guitar. These songs still resonate today when played at the right moments.

The first Beatle song that Neil Young learned to play was reputed to be 'Money'. This is a real rocking number delivered in full force on the 'Revolver' album and when Neil Young played 'A Day in the Life' at his Hyde Park concert in 2008, he was joined on stage by Paul McCartney who put his arm around Neil's shoulder and accompanied him on the vocals. These two veterans of that long musical odyssey that started for both of them in the sixties stood there delivering the goods as they always had done. They both have an amazing output of material and they have surely had many common experiences. Working as performers during the sixties when elements of what they created had an immeasurable influence on people's lives. As the Irish say 'They have known the days'. And those were the days when performers socialized backstage at gigs and TV shows. In this way they interacted artistically plus the social commitment of many bands influenced many things we take for granted today. From the beginning the Beatles refused to play segregated stadiums in the South because as they said *"we owe everything to Black music."*

Neil Young had his stance against the War in Vietnam. These actions have been underrated in our present day assessment of the role of these bands in the sixties. They were entertainers but they also had ideals that they lived up to. Larry Kane who toured with the Beatles on their first major American tour as a reporter said:

"Before them, it was unheard of for a rock group to get politically involved in any way. After the Beatles, and especially due to Lennon's public activism, scores of popular music icons follow the lead, and they continue to do so. The Beatles role in this synergy of music and protest has been largely ignored by historians of the era".[51]

7. The American influence on the Beatles

The whole 'ping pong' effect of the American and British experience needs to be examined more closely. The first close contact of any consequence the Brits had with Yanks was during WW2. The country was overrun with American troops and Air bases, 'over paid over sexed and over here' was the common lament at the time. Despite this that generation was eternally grateful for the sacrifice made by the Americans during that conflict. Later in London when Hendrix was confronted by angry veterans for publicly wearing military jackets he would often get a pat on the back after he had told them that he had served in the 101 Airborne.[52] This regiment had taken heavy losses on D-Day in 1944 and that had not been forgotten by the generation that went through the war. But it was very hard for this self-same generation who had lived through the Second World War to see their hard earned values and ideals diminishing in the sixties as the British Empire crumbled and young people started to focus on having fun. A good example of this situation can be seen in the film "A Hard Day's night" in the opening scene in the train carriage where and older gentleman of military bearing is offended by one of Ringo's remarks and reprimands him ;

"Don't take that tone with me, young man. I fought the war for your sort". To which Ringo replies *"I bet you're sorry you won."*[53]

Another connection was during the post war years thousands of GI's were stationed in Europe, throughout the Cold War. They had their own radio station 'AFN' (American Forces Network) where local populations could also hear on their transistor radios music that was popular in America. Jazz, Blues and early Rock and Roll records were brought over by merchant seamen and personal working on the Liners between the States and Britain who were known locally as 'Cunard Yanks'. Especially in sea ports like Liverpool and Hamburg these records went through a system of bartering and swapping. The records would eventually find their way into the hands of aspiring Skiffle groups like Lennon's 'Quarrymen'.[54] Skiffle can be compared to Bluegrass in respect that it was an offshoot from Country music and the Blues. This can be clearly heard in songs like 'Pick a Bail of Cotton' a Leadbelly number covered by Lonnie Donegan. The Skiffle sound round Britain was characterized by regions. Ringo stated that Liverpool was commonly known among bands as the 'Nashville of the North' and its brand of Skiffle was called 'Western Skiffle' because of the Country and Western influence. This influence would later become evident in Beatle songs like the songs on 'Help' which accompanied the release of their second film.

The track selection on Help was different on the British and American copies plus the American version of their next album 'Rubber Soul' had two acoustic tracks from the UK version of Help that were not on the American copy; 'I've Just seen a Face' and 'It's Only love'. By adding these additional tracks the PR people at Capitol records gave the American version of Rubber Soul a more cohesive folk rock sound that was dominating the American market at that time. This practice really infuriated the Beatles who carefully selected the tracks on their albums and avoided number that had been singles. However in the USA business came before artistic endeavor. This practice did enable Capitol to increase the popularity of the Beatles in America by releasing six albums in 1965 compared to the four albums EMI released in Britain.

Bill Wyman who was doing National service in Germany in the late 1950's was hearing records by Chuck Berry and Little Richard a year before they were released in Britain.[55] Records could be bought by American servicemen in their PX stores and ended up on juke boxes in Germany or were passed on to friends. Some years later the reverse would happen with Neil Young's 'Squires' in Winnipeg. Canada had always had a special relationship to the UK because many people still had family connections there. Through these connections Neil Young was able to get records by UK bands like the Shadows.

Most of the young men in Skiffle groups came from the working classes, growing up in slums and council houses, they were factory fodder segregated at 11 years old by the '11 plus' exam. Those that failed went on to secondary schools and had prospects in life (especially in the North of England) of ship yards, factory jobs or coal mines. That's how it had been for generations the war had taken their fathers around the world and a career in the Military or Merchant Navy was still one of the only ways of getting out. As Pete Townsend stated:

"The Army was the straight guys acid."

It was one of the only ways for working class boys to change their lives. Many young men followed the traditions of their father and grandfathers by walking through the factory gates in the morning. Many of them had got their girlfriends pregnant and married young. They stood at machines all day long and fell into a rut of routine that would seldom be broken. The Beatles song 'Girl' from that time sums up the situation perfectly:

"Was she told when she was young that pain would lead to pleasure? Did she understand them when they said? That a man must break his back to earn his day of leisure."

Young guys could relate to this and wanted to break the cycle. The boom of pop music groups performing and making records in the sixties created another viable way for working class lads to earn a living. I do not propose that all bands in the UK were from the working class but they were in the majority contrarily to the United States where many bands like the Byrds, The Doors, Bob Dylan and others mainly came from middle class backgrounds. As their ranks swelled in the UK these groups composed of enthusiastic young men learnt the new songs with a passion, playing in pubs and clubs, exchanging songs, records and ideas. They enjoyed the act of breaking away from the confines of a conventional working class career and savoured the success as music became a focal point in the society. As a teenage fan going to a concert you left the post war semidetached two up two down behind you and were transformed to another place. Surrounded by laughter and commotion where people gelled in the anticipation of having a good time. Young people got a feeling of joy and freedom from a night out just having a ball in a spacious brightly lit dance hall away from the dark, dank streets of post war Britain. You only have to look at the two films of UK tours in 1965 by Bob Dylan[56] and later one by the Rolling Stones[57] to see how drab it all really was. There is almost nothing happening on the streets and they were still using horses and carts!

Britain was really poor as Trevor Davis points out in his film 'A Time and the City', in 1953 at the time of Queen Elizabeth II coronation: *"A large part of the British population were living in some of the most appalling slums in the whole of Europe"*.

The vitality of Rock and Roll music that came from America with the jeans and boots, cokes and leather jackets was something young Brits aspired to. The influence of the rebellious life style that Marlon Brando and James Dean championed in American movies can be seen in the early Beatles photos in Hamburg. Posing in leather jackets and jeans with Brylcreemed hair brushed back in the popular American DA style. Paul McCartney protested that the film 'Back Beat' was historically inaccurate because it did not portray him in a leather jacket like the rest of the Beatles. Historical accuracy in semi documentary films like these is obviously important to people like 'Macca' who wants history to remember him as one of the lads back in Hamburg and not some twat. Films were a big influence in the 1950's and 60's on the young generation. Aside from the fact in the UK the cinema was one of the few places one could take a date and have some seclusion in the back row. American movies were far racier than the ones made by British studios and people flocked to see them. It was a stroke of genius that Epstein used American directors for both the Beatles films. This definitely gave them an edge in giving them an American dimension that appealed to the British public. The British invasion reintroduced Rock and Roll to America with a Twist (no pun intended), the very strong regional accents and in many cases very, very young stars compared to many of the top American entertainers at the time. Cheerful, lively and cocky, good at their trade, bands like Herman's Hermits, the Searchers, Hollies, Dave Clark Five and Jerry and the Pacemakers, charmed the US public. British bands got inspiration from their tours of America, the speed of life over there and the abundance of consumer products. Radio and TV shows and cities that never seemed to sleep.

The Beatles picked up commonplace words in America like 'Ticket to Ride', 'Day Tripper' and 'Paperback Writer' that sounded exotic to English ears. Another aspect was that the American journalists encouraged by the Beatles outspokenness on almost all subjects started asking all celebrities questions about politics and current social issues, whereas in Britain previously it had just been mundane things like *"Do you prefer Blondes or Brunettes?"* or *"What's your favourite drink?"*

This new dimension the Beatles took home with them along with inspiration from people like David Crosby and Peter Fonda who coming from far more affluent backgrounds had that distinctly American outlook that anything was possible. For many young Americans of that generation the world was their oyster. This must have been quite a revelation to the Beatles with their tea and biscuits in the front room upbringing. One has to remember that Britain was very repressive at that time after going through a horrible war of rationing and destruction. Schools were run on along archaic disciplinary lines where everyone was addressed by their surnames. Corporal punishment continued in schools in the UK for decades after it was banned in the rest of Europe.

Artists like David Crosby and Gram Parsons of the Byrds were coming from a completely different place. Crosby grew up in a house where his dad used an Oscar award as a door stop. Parson had a financial allowance that made him financially independent. Dylan was reputed to have an allowance from his family and Peter Fonda's dad was the famous Henry Fonda. Crosby befriended the Beatles early in their career and he can be seen on YouTube in the background at some of the Beatles first US press conferences. He followed them on some legs of their tours and is said to have given George Harrison his first Indian instrument. These examples show an interaction and emergence between two youth cultures, sharing a common language but coming from vastly different backgrounds with a completely different set of rules concerning how to live and what was possible. This contrast in culture despite sharing a common language is quite astounding; on one side of the Atlantic you had rich and prosperous USA that had suffered no bomb damage during WW2. On the other side there was England with its still visible bomb sites in London and an economy drained by the war. It was a bleak, drab, grey environment.

 A good example of the fugal attitude that dominated even in government at that time is when the 'Blue Streak' rocket scientists visited the US to take part in a conference they cabled Whitehall to ask permission to rent a car and were told to rent bicycles!

London was smog, a pint of Bitter, Woodbine cigarettes and Ford Angelia's. It slowly started to swing after the Beatles Royal Command Performance at the London Palladium in 1963. The Beatles at that time were towing the line under the auspices of Brian Epstein. They were working hard at becoming the world's best Rock and Roll band. Epstein did not interfere with the musical side of things but he put them in suits and insisted on good manners. He turned them into lovable mop tops. After the initial American tours of 1964, 1965, 1966 more than just the veneer on their Epiphone guitars was starting to peel off. The album 'Rubber Soul' was a giant leap forward in the Beatles musical vision. Released at the end of 1965 it were the first studio album they had made without touring and other commitments to interrupt their work. Brian Wilson said it was the first pop music album he had heard that did not sound as if it was a compilation of hit songs with other songs used as fillers.

The US release of Rubber Soul had a different track compilation giving it a much more folk rock feel that accommodated the emerging American genre that was spearheaded by the Byrds and Bob Dylan. On the back of the cover George Harrison is even dressed as a Cowboy. As Paul McCartney said Rubber Soul was clearly a departure from the poppy stuff they had been doing up to then and John Lennon stated it was here that the Beatles started to take more control in the studio.

The working focus in the future would be on the albums the Beatles were making. This was evident with their next album the phenomenal musically ground-breaking 'Revolver'. Most Rock musicians agree that this album became a catalyst for the subsequent sounds of rock music. The sounds produced by revolutionary engineering techniques (at least in the pop music genre) showed what was possible. Although the song 'Tomorrow Never Knows' sounds relatively tame these days, in 1966 nothing like it had ever been heard before on the commercial airwaves. It sounded like something from another world. Pop music was slowly evolving into a serious art form.

The music became more and more sophisticated and experimental until it culminated in 1967 with the Beatles masterpiece 'Sergeant Pepper's Lonely Hearts Club Band'. At the time of its release in the UK Paul McCartney was producing the Monterey Pop Festival together with Mark Philips of the Mamas and Papas. The organizers of the festival had been anxious about putting on a festival of popular music. Would it be accepted as a serious art form like Classical and jazz? When McCartney went to the states he took with him acetate of the Sgt. Pepper album. The arrangers were some of the first people to hear it over there. With Sgt. Peppers the Beatles had yet again moved the boundaries and set a new benchmark for what could be achieved.

Neil Young should have performed at Monterey. He was on the bill with Buffalo Springfield but like other occasions before and after he derailed the train. Neil Young always follows his muse regardless of the cost or consequences. In the final analysis he will always go his own way and his fans love him for it. A classic example came later in his career with the success of 'Harvest' instead of repeating the winning formula he "headed for the ditch". Luck seemed to play a big part in what happened to a lot of performing artists at that time. Concerning Buffalo Springfield Neil Young and Stephen Stills were by no means just lucky being in the right place at the right time. They were both accomplished musicians when they formed the band, performing since their early teens in high school bands. While they were growing up solo artists dominated the music scene. For example in 1960 there were only 20 bands in the billboard 100 chart. Three years later that number doubled to 40, the year after that in 1964 the British invasion struck. Spearheaded by the Beatles, British bands occupied 26 places in the US charts. Twelve of the compositions were by Lennon and McCartney. At one time the Beatles filled the top four slots on the Billboard 100.

The era of the band dawned exactly when Neil Young and Stephen Stills were impressionable young men and the market was ripe for groups in the US who were fighting to correct the imbalance. The Beatles became teen idols worldwide and the term 'Beatlemania' became universal to describe the phenomena. The Buffalo Springfield did not however have the lengthily experience of playing together as a unit that the Beatles had. As individuals they had been in touring small clubs for a couple of years playing in various small bands. This could not compensate for the fact they were still only 19 years old, while that may appear to be very young today one must remember that many of their contemporaries at that age were being shipped off to Vietnam. They formed Buffalo Springfield but were not destined to make it big 'that time around'. A little older and wiser when they formed CSN&Y who after their appearance at Woodstock went up like a rocket filling stadiums and airways. CSN&Y opened the floodgates for a host of Californian bands. In all fields of human endeavour it is in human nature to compete for the leading slot. Ambitious people will always strive to be bigger and better than the best. This natural instinct encouraged many young American bands not only to counter attack the British invasion but to try and be better than the Beatles. With the Beatles decision to break up made public in April 1970, Bill Graham said that CSN&Y had achieved that goal.

The fact is CSN&Y were the only American band to come close to the social impact that the Beatles had. After the British invasion bands became the dominant factor on the American music scene. I do not propose that the British invasion started the trend of music groups in the States as the charts show bands were on the increase in America during the sixties. However the invasion did increase the presence of bands in the charts by 100% and that was an inspiration to aspiring musicians like Roger Guinn, David Crosby, Stephen Stills and Neil Young who wanted to be in bands. Dylan had befriended the Beatles and is credited with introducing them to recreational drugs. They in turn acknowledge Dylan's songs as a source of inspiration. Neil Young and Jimi Hendrix both give Dylan credit as an inspiration to sing in their own idiosyncratic voices, which at that time were very different to the conventional sounds of a lead vocalist in a pop group. As Hendrix put it in a letter to his father:

 "Nowadays people don't want you to sing good. They want you to sing sloppy and have a good beat to your song. So that's what angle I'm going to shoot at".[58]

When Country Rock started to appear after the mid-sixties there was a common bond among young people who were into artists like Neil Young and Bob Dylan and bands like Buffalo Springfield and The Byrds. These musicians consciously or unconsciously became role models for young people. Many of these young people were looking for guidance to find a way-out of the confines and restrictions of the conventional lifestyle put on them by their parents and a society. For many people the lyrics of pop songs became an inspiration. Elvis Presley represented the Rock and Roll rebellion both in style and sound.

He sounded black and he moved like no-one had seen before, John Lennon said, *"before Elvis there was nothing."* Jim Morrison was equally spellbound by the man who would be King. This mixture of Gospel, Rhythm and Blues and Rock and Roll that came out of America was embraced by the Beatles who added the dimension of British Skiffle which gave them an edge. It gave them a new distinct fresh sound. Like Dylan said no-one was playing the chord sequences and harmonies that the Beatles were doing at that time. For people who are not familiar with the Beatles it is a good idea to start around the time of the LP 'Beatles for Sale 'and the single 'Ticket to Ride' then go on to 'Help' where traces of Country and Western influence start to appear in their records.

The early Beatlemania that swept through the US during the first wave of the British invasion seemed to show something else. Firstly it was mainly female and secondly the music seemed to come second to the adulation of the actual members of the band. The Beatle records released in Britain up to 'Revolver' were vastly different to the American releases that were put together by Capitol specifically for the American market. Beatlemania was something previously unseen and during that period, everything was a novelty for the Beatles as they travelled the world and were met by large crowds of fans at every airport. The lucky fans that got to see them live in concert went home after the show and continued their lives much as before but now 'in love with a Beatle' and the record sales soared. The Beatles music and the music of the counter culture in 1967 started searching for more spiritual direction and a more reflective approach to appreciating the music.

This can also be seen in Neil Young's elaborate orchestral accompaniment to his songs on Buffalo Springfield's second album called 'Again'. The music became something you *"got into"* as Graham Nash explained; *"In those days you bought a record took it home, you rolled a big joint, took the foil off the record, put it on the record player then really got into the music."*[59] That's what happened with Crosby Stills and Nash records and other records that originally only appealed to the counter culture. What happened at festivals was comparable to the Indians smoking a peace pipe and passing it around. This spiritual searching caused a boom in the West for interest in Eastern religions. Ravi Shankar played at Monterey and Woodstock he had previously inspired George Harrison who incorporated the sitar into the Beatles music on Revolver and Sgt. Peppers. David Crosby is credited for turning George Harrison on to Ravi Shankar. This is a further illustration how the musicians inspired each other and crossed paths musically. Graham Nash had sat on the stage singing harmonies to 'All You Need is love' as it was beamed around the world by satellite.

Allen Ginsberg had incorporated Buddhism and Mantras into his work. People meditated in parks and at festivals. Great things occurred on both side of the Atlantic. The Monterey Pop Festival was a ground breaking moment putting popular music on the map as a serious art form and expression of a generation that identified with it. The relevance of the success of the Monterey Pop Festival should not be underestimated. Before Monterey there had only been festivals of 'serious' music like Classical and Jazz. 'Monterey Pop' could just as easily have turned out to be 'Monterey Flop' and music festivals would have ended there, but because of its success the British followed by organizing the first Isle of Wight Festival, (1968) booking top acts like Hendrix, Dylan and the Who. This would happen repeatedly during the sixties, the status quo in the entertainment industry could not predict the trends in films and music. The market demands dictated the direction and film directors and musicians in the entertainment business supplied the demand. Low budget films like "Easy Rider" and Spaghetti Westerns achieved success compatible with the big budget movies made in Hollywood. Musical artists took more control over the production of their work. The roles were in many cases reversed instead of producers directing musical bands and orchestras as they had done in the past. Rock artists and other performers dictated to producers the sound they wanted to create. Ever since the early days of Rock bands like the Beatles, Stones and The Jimi Hendrix Experience always gave their sound priority over their dress style and fashion image.

This became even more evident as the bands became more and more involved with the mixing and producing of their own records. Neil Young and Stephen Stills were not satisfied with the production of their first Buffalo Springfield album and decided they had to learn more about the technical production process of recording. Neil Young had a recording studio built into the cellar of his house in 1968. Private recording studios became the norm among the rock elite. Traditional recording studios and methods of production appeared confining and in some cases technically inadequate. Hendrix designed his state of the art recording studio 'Electric Ladyland' in New York to accommodate his recording ambitions. This enterprise nearly broke him financially and because of this he was forced to continue a grueling schedule of live dates.

The Beatles stopped touring at the time of Sergeant Peppers to totally dedicate themselves to creating music in the studios. For their creative endeavours they had unlimited access to EMI's recording studio. Bob Dylan booked a studio in Nashville for a 14 day block to record his masterpiece 'Blonde on Blonde'. This had never been done before and the slightly amazed session musicians sat around playing cards and smoking cigarettes while Bob finished off writing songs. They grabbed what sleep they could in between takes. This autonomy spread into other areas of the entertainment industry when actors like Jack Nicholson and Clint Eastwood achieved prominence, they stared producing and directing their own films. Up until that time plastics and synthetics were all the rage and dominated fashion and design in mainstream culture. Now something started happening in the entertainment industry where people were no longer willing to be puppets or marionettes, artificial elements in the construction of their work. They wanted to take charge of their own destiny even at the expense of losing popularity as was the case with the Monkees whose record sales plummet when they started to insist on playing their own instruments. After they turned down 'Sugar Sugar' it was recorded by the Archies a totally synthetic animated cartoon band. After that the Monkees lost their position as one of the top bands in the US. The counter culture started to associate more and more with natural products and authenticity. Many young people started to prefer clothes made from natural materials tie dyed by hand. The Beatles sanded down their Epiphone guitars to give a natural wood finish on the Revolver album.

The British invasion was a major factor to changing the format from solo artists to groups in the States. Giving the opportunity for musicians like Neil Young and Stephen Still's to form a band and 'get on the bandwagon.'

8. Frontier Spirit and the Buffalo

The parallels between the hippie / counter culture lifestyle and the frontier spirit are quite thought provoking. In all the old Westerns people were always packing up and moving on in covered wagons. Drifters like 'Shane' were always hitting town looking for something to tide them over but seldom seeking something more permanent. Some were searching for a new life and some were just looking for a new break. The mass immigration from Europe to the States was not based on the scenery over there but the chance of a better existence. Here is the crux of the problem, the Native Americans worshipped the land saw it as the mother. For them there was not a difference between the earth and the sky. They could not understand the concept of actually buying tracts of land and keeping it. It is said that when white settlers bought Manhattan Island for 12 horses the Indians asked them how much they would be willing to pay for the sky.

Europeans have always seen land as something you had to own. It must be conquered and cultivated and exploited for its natural resources. Up to the 21st century we destroyed the rain forests and pollute the oceans without really considering the consequences to future generations. Buffalo were shot to make way for herds of domestic cattle and deprive the Indians of the source of food that kept them independent. The Buffalo had mythological status and great spiritual meaning as well as material value to the Native Americans. Every part of the slain creature was used for clothes and food. When Buffalo herds were no longer a part of the American landscape they became a romantic image that still lingers in the collective memory of most Americans when they think of the Old West. This is one of Neil Young's strengths through his lyrics he is able to make us recollect these scenes and put them into some kind of context that we recognize. He can take a daily occurrence like someone's retirement as he does in the song 'Southern Pacific.'[60] Mr. Jones an ageing train driver is forced to go on pension when his eyesight starts to fail. Here the listener gets a nostalgic view of a man's working life being terminated and a lifestyle that is slowly disappearing. The Native Americans practiced Ghost Dancing in the belief that the Buffalo herds and the freedom they represented would return. This majestic beast is now only prominent in Native American mythology. Buffalo Bill kept a small herd on his ranch and Neil Young continues the tradition by keeping a small herd on his ranch. If one observes them in their natural habitat Buffalo are majestic creatures that one cannot help but associate with the 'Old West.'

9. The Wild West re-emerges in the sixties

From the mid-sixties to early seventies Country Rock Bands like Buffalo Springfield and Neil Young in particular used historical regalia. If you divide American history into two periods; the pre American civil war and post American civil war. The Country Rock bands of the sixties did not model their style on these legends of the "Wild Frontier" like Daniel Boone from 1734 or Davey Crockett and Jim Bowie, who both died at the Alamo 1836. The main area of inspiration for the American Country Rock groups was from the second half of the 19th century the period that was still within living memory known as the Old West or Wild West. This history covers geographically the United States west of the Mississippi River. This was the last area to be settled by Europeans as they pushed the Native Americans further westwards. In simplified terms: treaties were signed between the colonizing Europeans and the Native Americans to ensure peace. These treaties enabled Europeans to populate and cultivate vast areas of the North American continent without hindrance. As the European population increased at times doubling and tripling over a few years more land was needed and could only be taken from the Native Americans. This was justified in the eyes of the Europeans because a large proportion of Native Americans were not developing the land. They were nomads who only used the land for hunting and as far as the Europeans were concerned they could do that anywhere. They rationalized that if you fed Native Americans they could live on infertile land with no game. These arguments were used to push the boundaries further west breaking treaties and causing conflicts. When the Native Americans retaliated by attacking both illegal settlers and trespassing gold diggers military action was always justified to protect the whites. These actions did not respect the rights of the Native Americans. The resulting 'Indian War' would be settled by a 'peace treaty' which would ultimately leave the Native Americans with more promises and less land than they originally had. Or as seen in the 'Trail of Tears' they would be relocated to a place unsuitable for human habitat.

This inhuman treatment of Native Americans is the theme of John Ford's eulogy to the Native American 'Cheyenne Autumn' where a group of Indians put on a reservation in the desert in intolerable conditions decide to defy the authorities and journey north to their homelands. In one of John Fords earlier films 'Fort Apache'[61] he shows the situation of the Native American in closing of the frontier period. In this film the Native Americans raided the US from hideouts in Mexico. In this way they could avoid capture and prolong the conflict. In September 1886 the last Apaches fighting to defend their way of life under the leadership of Geronimo became the last group of Native Americans to surrender.[62] There was a period of transition taking place when this film was made in 1948. For many of the Native American actors similar events to the ones portrayed in the film were still within living memory and many of the grand parents of the young people in the audience had grown up in the last century when the closing of the border was relatively recent history. This gave them a familiarity and understanding that lead to a special relationship to this film and the rest of Fords Calvary Trilogy.

This was quite unique because you associated with the film through your heritage. Between 1910 and 1920 the Wild West shows were slowly disappearing but Native Americans were still a part of your parent's life through parades and State fairs. Then during the late forties and fifties movies like Fort Apache appeared that had a familiarity about them and in some ways recent history became more popular. The reason for this could be that as life became more complicated during the 20th century. There developed a wave of nostalgia for a bygone era when life was simpler and in many cases more satisfied (at least as it was portrayed on the silver screen) This could be part of the explanation of why the Western genre became so dominant during the 1950's in films and TV shows.

10. Country and Western Authenticity

With the Indian wars over and the closing of the frontier, the wide open prairies slowly became fenced off and divided up. The arrival of the railroad made the long cattle drives obsolete and slowly the demand for working Cowboys in a leading industrial nation became limited. The opportunity of following a carefree career on the range all but disappeared. Despite this lack of vocation Cowboys still tried to maintain their "Lone Star" image by appearing at travelling shows like Cattle Markets, Rodeos and Country Fairs. The image of the Cowboy was kept alive to some extent by the country music genre which had its center in Nashville. Here traditional country music had its own music chart and radio station KWKH launched a country show 'Louisiana Hayride' to compete with the established Grand Old Opray radio station. The Hayride helped make Hank Williams a recording star and a young Elvis Presley appeared regularly opening for established country starts like the Carter Sisters and Hank Snow.[63] In the late 1940's and 1950's Hank Williams appeared on many sponsored radio shows like "The Health and Happiness Show" and 'Mothers Best Show'. These live shows now available on CD recreate the atmosphere from that time where people in the Southern States baked biscuits for breakfast and fetched the milk from the cows in the barn. These shows rejuvenated nostalgia for bygone days when life was simpler and people seemed to be closer, at least that is the impression you get hearing these shows today. In Nashville one of the main concert venues was the Grand Ole Opry that put on shows with famous country music celebrities like Roy Acuff, Hank Williams, Buck Owens and female artists like Loretta Lynn and the much loved 'Queen of Country' Patsy Cline whose greatest hits record stayed in the country charts for 722 weeks selling 10 million copies.[64] This puts the popularity of country music in a perspective that is sometimes not appreciated outside the US. Through internet media like YouTube more people are getting an insight into the magnitude of country music. There is a tendency to focus the tastes of the younger generation because they are targeted by the music industry and represented in the media on channels like MTV. But country music with stars like Glen Campbell was still immensely popular in the United States during the 1960's and was the only serious competition to the Beatles dominance of the US music charts. In the clothes and the songs country music was paying homage to a set of values and a way of living that had disappeared or was disappearing in America. Through the support of their fans throughout America country stars continued to shine. Nashville was the country music capitol where the best session musicians and recording engineers were based. The Beatles in turn had found inspiration in country music that was especially noticeable during their 'Help' period. It is well known that many of the UK bands in the sixties like the Beatles were inspired by Skiffle. What is not so well known is that "Pride of the Prairie" recorded by Billy Murray in 1907 on the Edison label was the first 'Cowboy Song' to become a hit in the British Isles. That was 33 years before Ringo Starr was born in Merseyside where 'Cowboy Music' was more prevalent than anywhere else in the UK.[65] Most probably due to transatlantic seamen who imported records by the American top artists in the early 1950's. Ringo recalls hearing songs like Hank Snow's "I am Movin On", Hank Thompson and his Brazo Valley Boys "The Wild Side of Life" and Buck Owens "Down on the Corner of Love." This influence became evident by the prominence of Skiffle groups around Liverpool that had a distinctive Country and Western flavour in the mid 1950's.

By 1955 the Liverpool Philharmonic Hall had more than 40 operational local 'Cowboy ' groups and by the end of the decade became known as the Nashville of the North.[66] Along with the Liverpool Philharmonic Hall there were 300 venues affiliated to the 'Liverpool Social Club Association' many of the Skiffle bands like Gerry Marsden's were too young to drink and modelled themselves on popular TV shows like 'Cheyenne' or 'Wagon Train' giving themselves names like: 'Clay Ellis and the Raiders', 'James Boys' and later 'Johnny Sandon and the Searchers' inspired by the classic John Ford movie "The Searchers". Despite this Country and Western heritage the Beatles never did play in Nashville on their American tours. After they disbanded Ringo recorded the country album 'Beaucoup of Blues' in Nashville with many veterans including Ben Keith (who later played with Neil Young). This record was not a commercial success but remained one of Ringo's personal favourites. During the sixties and early seventies Bob Dylan and Neil Young both recorded some of their major works there.

The Byrd's recorded their country rock classic 'Sweetheart of the Rodeo' in Nashville. By the mid-sixties many country artists like Glen Campbell who had a very clean cut image were considered rednecks by the hip generation. This stigma against country music was counter-attacked by Merle Haggard in the song 'Okie from Muskogee.' Still the 'Hip' generation preferred to cultivate the Beatles music and groups like them. John, Paul, George and Ringo had by now abandoned their loveable mop top image and adapted the longhaired guru look of 'Old Testament Prophets.'[67] The Beatles style of music was becoming more psychedelic and experimental. The texts had become more intrinsic with the lavish use of synonyms and the 'hip' language of the period contributing to what had become a mature poetic dialogue with the audience.

The Beatles were very much a product of their time. They were skilled musicians and master song writers but the influences that helped shape the music were not only internal. To a very large degree, external elements like Dylan and Hendrix contributed vastly to what many artists of that time, including Neil Young were doing. This type of evolution never really took place on a large scale within country music. The style and recording techniques became more sophisticated but the acoustic guitar and banjos accompanied by the steel and electric guitars were the mainstay of the country sound. This meant artists like Bob Dylan and Neil Young could always return to the genre during their careers without having to acclimatize themselves to new musical styles. The late great Johnny Cash was a permanent fixture in Country Music. He did many concept albums about American history and the Wild West in the early sixties[68] and Neil Young appeared several times with Johnny Cash on TV. Bob Dylan received a guitar from Johnny Cash; this was a tradition among folksingers as a symbol of recognition for the other artist. Dylan in turn invited Johnny Cash to play with him on his album 'Nashville Skyline'. Johnny Cash was proud of his Cherokee heritage, (he is said to have disclaimed this later).[69] As an artist he was very aware of the injustices meted out to the Native Americans and performed a show on the reservation at Wounded Knee.

Johnny Cash released the album 'Bitter Tears' that he co-wrote with Peter La Farge releasing the controversial single 'The ballad of Ira Hayes' in 1964. Dylan also covered this song on his 1973 album 'Bob Dylan (A Fool Such as I).' Ira Hayes a Pima Native American was one of five Marines who raised the American flag on Iwo Jima (he is the guy on the far left). He is buried in Arlington National Cemetery.[70] At the funeral, fellow flag-raiser Rene Gagon said of him: "*Let's say he had a little dream in his heart that someday the Indian would be like the white man and be able to walk all over the United States.*" The Marines supported another Native American, Billy Mills a Lakota Sioux who was took part in the NCAA cross country competitions from 1960 to 1963. Every year he was asked to step outside of championship pictures documenting runners in finishing slots even though sometimes he was the only American winner among the foreign students attending American schools. In 1963 he took part in the Amateur Athlete Union competition in Van Courtland Park, NY. Only this time he was representing the Marine Corps.

"When I was asked to step aside, after having finished third in the cross country championship race, the highest American ranked, the photographer was confronted by a Marine Corps officer. "Lieutenant Mills will not step out of the picture," the photographer was informed. "He is a Marine Corps officer". To make sure there was a complete understanding of the message, the officer proceeded to shake him. I got my picture taken."[71]

Later Billy Mills would win Gold in the 10,000 meters in Tokyo Olympics 1964. There was of course racism in the service just as there was in the society but it was in the Armed Forces some of the first changes came regarding equality and civil rights. As USMC general Carl Mundy said at a memorial service on Iwo Jima in November 1993:

"Were Ira Hayes here today.... I would tell him that although my words on another occasion have given the impression that I believe some Marines ... because of their color ... are not as capable as other Marines ... that those were not the thoughts of my mind ... and that they are not the thoughts of my heart."

Admitting one is wrong is a sign of real strength and general Mundy here gives a chance for reconciliation for some of the injustices done to ethnic minority groups who previously served. A quote from Billy Mills sums things up pretty well;

"What I took from the Olympic Games was not winning an Olympic gold medal but an understanding of global unity through dignity of character and pride of global diversity. And global unity through global diversity is also the future of mankind."[72]

The country and western acts from the previous decade like Gene Autry, Tex Ritter and Sons of the Pioneers identified strongly with the Cowboy image and cowboy songs as a genre thrived during the depression. During the 1930's Patsy Montana became the first female country artist to sell a million records with "I Wanna be a Cowboy Sweetheart."[73] The stage image of country artists of at that time was clearly meant to appear theatrical. Hank Williams was one of the originators of flashy Western attire, always looking sharp and very flamboyant in his Stetson hats and 'Nudie' suits that were later adopted by Gram Parson`s and the Flying Burrito Brothers.

One of the reasons country music stage costumes appeared more theatrical could be partly because Cowboys in their full working gear, ten gallon hats and chaps had become a seldom sight on the Streets of Laredo and the general populace were only exposed to the attire through the entertainment business. Later there emerged various re-enactment groups throughout the United States who became popular for staging historical battles and events from American history like the American Civil War. There is a visual affinity here with the West but they generally have a mental and physical distance from their costumes and the era they represent. It is very clear that they are "acting." In comparison, the dress from the Country Rock bands has been incorporated into mainstream fashion: jeans, cowboy boots, denim jackets, bandanas became mainstream casual dress.

A bandana is a good example of continuity together with jeans they are work clothing from one period in history that crosses over into another period of history transforming into leisure clothes. Like the ex-military jackets purchased from army surplus stores. The durability of military clothes and jeans made them especially attractive to young people who during the sixties started to shun traditional dress codes. So much so that the more worn out they looked the more coveted they became, Neil Young's patched jeans on the cover of "After the Goldrush" are a good example. Neil Young and other Country Rock artists tried to be authentic and rekindle some of the image and spirit of the Old West. They played laid back songs about sleeping in the desert under the stars, the idyllic life of the Cowboy and the romantic image of the Outlaw. The instruments they use in their music are Western Guitars and Banjos and Steel Guitars that fit the old period combined with contemporary instruments like Fender and Gibson electric guitars. They created a hybrid out of the two music forms.

The album covers were different they were not the studio portraits traditionally used by early Country and Western artists. The Country Rock groups LP covers depict scenes that were part of the 'collective visual memory': Remington paintings, John Ford movies, cowboys riding across empty deserts, old railroad shacks and Western towns with dusty streets. There was spontaneity and simplicity compared to the psychedelic flamboyance of many progressive rock album covers.

Country Music and Country and Western music has been very important and influential in American music, influencing Folk Music, Bluegrass and Rock Music which then had a major influence on music all over the world. Not least in Britain where the bands like the 'Quarrymen' who were the forerunners of the Beatles cut their teeth on Skiffle music. Country legend Hank Williams was one of the first to reach a wider audience with his enormous hit "Lovesick Blues" in 1948.[74] It is worth noting that like Presley with "Heartbreak Hotel" Hank Williams had to fight to get 'Lovesick Blues' recorded and in both cases the conviction of the artist paid off. There are many examples of continuality for example Neil Young has a guitar that belonged to Hank Williams that he plays at the grand Old Oprey in the movie 'Heart of Gold'.[75] Is that keeping the faith or just entertainer's superstition? Music is a spiritual thing and people read into it their own definitions. The band gives you its interpretation of how they perceive it and if it appeals to you it becomes accepted (if it appeals to everyone it becomes mainstream). This whole process takes time and for some bands like Buffalo Springfield there was not time enough.

11. Authenticity

The youth of the sixties demanded radical changes and liberation from the strict moral attitudes that had confined the previous generation. When fashion designers like Mary Quant launched the miniskirt from her shop 'Bazaar's' in the Kings Road London, the demand was bottom up (no pun intended). Mary Quant's parent's generation just wanted things to return to how they were before the Second World War. Mary Quant and other designers were looking towards the future and the demands of young people. That was their objective when they contributed to the creation of Swinging London and Mod fashion. London became the international center of the fashion world at that time. There were boutiques like 'Bazaar' and 'Lord Kitchener's Valet' among others situated in the Portobello Road and Carnaby Street where for the first time in the UK clothes were displayed on racks outside the shops.

London was literally buzzing with small clothes shops and flea markets where shoppers who finally had a bit more money to spend due to the economic upswing could pick and mix different items of clothes like antique military jackets made popular by artists like Jimi Hendrix and Eric Clapton. The hot spot for rock musicians relaxing in the mid-sixties was a basement off Masons Yard called the 'Scotch of St. James Club' another epicenter was the 'Bag of Nails' where Hendrix played the very night he arrived in England with Chas Chandler.

Popular music bands started to hold concerts at venues like the Royal Albert hall that had previously been bastions of classical music and opera. Other popular places for local and visiting bands were the Rainbow Theatre off Finsbury Park and the Marquee Club. Through the visual image of bands male dress became radically different. Rock stars walked around dressed like they would on stage very colourful and flamboyant. There were many Mod bands like the Who and the Kinks along with other performers like Jimi Hendrix and Mick Jagger and the Rolling Stones. They all donned long colourful scarfs and wore brightly coloured shirts and trousers with hats and an assortment of colourful boots and shoes clothes.

These styles especially when they were blatantly effeminate were often frowned upon by their peer groups who were still dressed in the confirmative suits and ties. But slowly their hair was growing over the collar and styles were changing. Girls were also provoking their boyfriends not to appear 'square'. All this promoted the modern fashion. You became identifiable from your peers. You were either 'with it' or without it. As Graham Nash said *"you would see someone with long hair and know that person appreciated good music and was into the things you were into"*. The African Americans in the Northern States where Jimi Hendrix came from wore sharp suits and dark glasses. They found it hard to relate to the guy in the feathered boa, wide hat, afghan jacket and velvet trousers. The reception in San Francisco was different there the Hippy dress style was a common sight on the streets. The pink suits and effeminate style of Mick Jagger and Brian Jones got a lot of flak in the UK from young working class males and the Stones were constantly targets for insults and abuse by the press in countries like Australia where macho journalists often asked provoking questions like: *"Don't you feel like a poof dressed like that?"*

Through their images musicians played an immense role in defining the fashion that became popular. They promoted clothes intentionally or unintentionally by wearing them at press conferences and while performing. Their actions helped to legalize the kind of outrageous dress that previously would have got people committed in the UK. This is a very crucial point in regards to the sixties; before this time men wore dark nondescript suits and the only colour of shirts was white. Women only wore dresses and skirts that generally went below the knee, and black or brown shoes. As Country Joe commented on an interviewers clothes when he was asked if Woodstock had really changed anything: *"Before what happened in the sixties you could not have worn a shirt like that"*.

Pop stars had the economic clout to change the status quo. Hendrix was purported to have paid £300 for his old Hussars dress jacket (this jacket was later identified as a veterinarians dress jacket) at that time factory workers earned about £6 a week. Groups like Jefferson Airplane and Janis Joplin were doing the same in the States. Janis Joplin especially broke away from the traditional way of matching ladies clothing where your handbag matched the rest of your attire. She championed the idea of people wearing what they felt good in. These influences went back and forth across the Atlantic. Music crossed borders in the form of gifts and promotional copies before their official release in different countries. The clothes and styles were seen by young people in films and on record covers and soon spread throughout the West. Pictures of the British actress Julie Christie appeared in the media when she returned from the US clad from head to toe in fringed buckskins.

This is the point that James Mazzeo made that fashion and style is not necessarily associated with the Native American culture or values when you look at Neil Young. Despite everything else Neil Young is performer. He goes on stage to deliver a show. He has a role to play along with his occupation as a musician. He is a child of his time and he is going along with what is going on around him. In the early days groups like the Beatles, Stones, Kinks and the Who all dressed very sharp and in the tradition of what became the Mods in the UK. Similarly in the US early pictures of Buffalo Springfield have echoes of the London Mods fashion. In the booklet accompanying the Buffalo Springfield box set they can be seen wearing suits and Neil is in brightly designed sweaters, Chelsea boots and slacks. Neil Young incorporated the Comanche War jackets into his image. Being a young man in white slacks, polo neck and boots he thought he was 'pretty hot'.[76] Consciously or unconsciously all these bands slowly attached themselves to the progressive rock faction that was becoming more and more comfortable in jeans and T-shirts. The main ethos here was that the music was the main thing and any flashy stage presence was secondary.

 The trend of not giving bands a uniformed appearance started during the mid-sixties was later illustrated on the cover of the Beatles 'Abbey Road'. The band is dressed individually in three different coloured suits and George Harrison is dressed completely in denim. There is no doubt that the counter cultures adoption of Native American images created a growing awareness in the sixties for the Native American culture. Neil Young became a part of this trend through his use of Comanche war jackets. He was reputed to have been one of the originators when the image is seen in connection with music groups. James Mazzeo points out "I was living in Haight Ashbury 1965-66 and lots of hippies were wearing Indian jewelries and accessories...moccasins and such."

Neil Young was right there when it was becoming 'cool' to be an Indian and this is one of my main contentions that this spread of the fashion in the Hippy community vastly contributed to general awareness. Commercially they created a demand and through various means the market came up with the supply; starting with small scale street vendors and independent companies making their own products to the more exclusive fashion orientated boutiques catering to actresses like Cher and Julie Christy and musicians like Neil Young. At both ends of the scale there was a buzz of creativity in the air combined with a genuine feeling of sharing that characterized the period. In a radio interview about her musical memories[77] in Copenhagen Annette who owned the poster shop 'Superlove' in Copenhagen during the sixties mentions that she was called by one of her friends a concert organizer to ask if she could pick up Jimi Hendrix from the airport? There wasn't any need for the massive security back then and to illustrate the feeling of sharing there was in the sixties she says: " *I got a shipment of posters from the States and one of the boxes was just 'topped up' with LP's from bands like the Doors and Jefferson Airplane that people here did not know at that time. So we had all these great sounds playing in the shop that no one had heard before.*"

These are the incidents people recall when they look back to that period, examples of genuine sharing. The person who put the records in the box was probably not thinking about the commercial aspect of what they were doing. They were sharing the intellectual experience, turning someone on who lived on the other side of the planet, to something that they really thought was really far out. It was a "Get a load of this man" kind of thing'. The phrase "Far Out" became the standard expression to everything that was going on at the time. These were the sixties and for the first time young people are 'running the show.' They could afford it because from 1959 to 1963 wages rose 70% while actual prices only increased 40%. Youth were spending considerably more than their parents could ever afford on clothes and entertainment, especially music. They gave music an unprecedented status, buying music, sharing music, going to concerts and festivals this created intense energy of immense creative activity, designing clothes, putting on shows, diversifying, crossing cultural boundaries, creating music that incorporated different genres and styles; Country and Western, Jazz and Rock. In the case of Buffalo Springfield it was country rock. Along with bands like the Byrds and Gram Parsons, they went back and forth into country and folk music. The Byrds sang Dylan songs, Gram Parsons hung out with Keith Richards in France at the time of "Exile on a Main Street" rekindling the Stones guitarists love of country music. This is a clear example of how the bands and musical artists of different styles interacted. By playing on each other's albums, sitting in on sessions and jamming together. It was the spirit of the times and it was carried along by an unprecedented economic boom.

In 1967 the UK economy was hit by a devaluation that was not noticeable among young people on the street. The boys about town strutted around in Mod gear while the Hippies headed for Kathmandu. For the first time ordinary working families were able to afford charter holidays abroad. It was the dawning of a new age. People experienced different ways of life, fashions and cultures. This in turn inspired different ways of doing things and gave many people a different outlook on how to lead their lives. In many ways tolerance became a major theme of the sixties and acceptance of differences in society especially in youth culture and gender issues. This change of outlook became visible in many forms, young people vented their pent up frustrations by demonstrating in the streets. Large portions of society started to demands changes. They had long been suppressed by rules and regulations upheld by intolerant authoritarian regimes. These outdated institutions fought to maintain the status quo but in the 1960's the floodgates opened and a flow or irreversible changes poured through. You can argue the pros and cons of the counter culture and if there really was a revolution. But without a doubt after 1960's the general populace had a better quality of life and much more self-determination about how they chose to live their lives.

12. Country Music

The origins of Country Music came from the Deep South. The sound migrated to Northern California in waves. The first wave was described by John Steinbeck in his book 'Grapes of Wrath'. Woody Guthrie and later Bruce Springsteen wrote a song about the main character Tom Joad who was portrayed by Henry Fonda in the film. The story is set in the1920´s depression period known as the 'dustbowl' when peoples left the poverty of rural Oklahoma to seek work fruit picking in California. The second wave came during the 1940's with the migration of munitions workers from the Southern States during WW2. Because of their requests to local radio stations country music got more exposure and became more popular. The American forces radio (AFN) was broadcast for military personal serving outside the US during the 1950´s. The station contributed vastly to inspiring early rhythm and blues fans in the UK and Germany. It exposed people like Bill Wyman (doing national service in Germany) to Country music along with Beat and 'Rock and Roll'. Country and Western music has not achieved the success of Soul music and Tamla Motown outside the US partly because the Blues and Jazz that they are based on has a universal appeal. 'The Wild West' or 'Old West' is a phenomena or period special to the United States. People outside could mimic it but not really feel a part of it. European culture is based on debates and discourse, whereas a cowboy's life seems to follow serendipity and the occasional 'Yup'. This is of course a bit of an understatement but there is an element of truth in it. The ethos of the cowboy was to take life as it comes. They drove the cattle, spent their wages and never seemed to settle down. TV shows like 'Wagon Train' and 'Rawhide' promoted this image of a cowboy's carefree life on the open prairies. Country and Western music had immense popularity in the US but not so much in the UK. Over there the TV shows were excepted and loved but the music hit the wrong note (no pun intended). For example one of the founding fathers of country music Jimmie Rodgers did not have much appeal to the UK audience. They found the country and western accents of many performers and especially the yodeling exaggerated. As can be seen in songs like 'Riding the Navajo Trail'. This could be partly due to the fact that the European audience had experienced bebop from guitarists like Django Reinhardt in the 1930-40's and found they had more empathy with Blues artists like John lee Hooker, Leadbelly and B.B. King. The American audience had the advantage of a genuine cultural reference point in country music, especially in the Southern States where they could identify with radio shows like Louisiana Hayride and the Grand Old Opray. Many of the aspects of these shows became associated with wholesome living. The folksy communal aspect had many parallels with vaudeville and music hall genre in the UK which gave an alternative to the highbrow music of the middle and upper classes. The formula was the same, presenters displayed familiarity with the performers and appeared sincere as they invited the audience to share an evening's entertainment of music and dance. Especially in the US where television gave the atmosphere of a Barn Dance or Hoe Down in your own living room making you a part of the audience. You felt like you were sharing an intimate moment or just sitting on your back porch talking to friends. They were speaking a language you could understand and playing songs that reflected the joys and hardships of working people's daily lives.

Previous to Television becoming widespread the radio was the main form of entertainment in ordinary households and radio shows played a key role in the family programs. The Carter Family, Jimmie Rodgers, Roy Acuff and Hank Williams had all been on radio shows. Down the years these entertainers have bought joy to millions of fans who appreciated them as their kind of people singing songs about experiences in life they could relate to. This made a bond with the audience who were sometimes fortunate to have experienced them in a live concert appearance. They felt like they knew the artist personally and loved them for the fact that they shared something with them. They came from the same country roots and knew one another's hometowns. Throughout his long career Neil Young has evoked the same kind of familiarity with his loyal fans, who have followed him from album to album. His dark horse mood swings have only endeared him more to their hearts as his music became part of the soundtrack to their lives.

When he was in Buffalo Springfield and CSN&Y these bands represented the 'Country Rock' sound in a form that was so special and unique it eventually acquired a universal appeal. It has to be appreciated that Country music plays an important part in Neil Young's life. He might wander into other musical genres at various stages in his career but he always seems to return to country music at some point. The lifestyle it evokes is what he appears to try and communicate to his fans and live audiences around the world. He might get caught up in the furore of what is happening around him and lash out with loud abrasive electric guitar chords like a cowboy shooting up the town. But in the end the sun always goes down and the cowboy saddles his horses to calmer tones of Martin guitar and banjo. Songs like 'Long walk Home'[78] where social political comment is combined with the refrain "It's such a long walk home" give the song a universal appeal that everyone can relate to, because at some time or another we have all watched a big parade or missed the last bus and taken that long walk home.

13. Country Rock Dress Style

The post-civil war period to the end of the century is the period the country rock dress style focused on. This was the time when the American Old West passed into history, the myths of the Wild West took firm hold in the imagination of Americans and immigrants alike. 'Go West Young man' became the slogan of the period encouraging people to head out West in Wagon Trains in search of their fortunes and to populate the wide open spaces. A good illustration of the difference between the East coast and the 'Wild West' can be seen in Jim Jarmusch's film 'Dead Man' (1995) with music by Neil Young. You see Johnny Depp as he travels by train across the American continent from a civilized Eastern world through to the uncultivated wilderness of the west. On his journey you can clearly see the transition from the urban landscape and the different types of passengers boarding the train as it heads into the West and the area known as the Great Plains. Each time he wakes up from his dozing the people around him have become more primitive as if he is also travelling back in time. Finally we see hunters in furs shooting Buffalo from the train windows just for fun. Many Country Rock bands adopted the style from the period known as the 'Wild West' that was legendary for its notorious outlaws like Jesse James, Billy the Kid, Dalton Brothers and popular figures like Wyatt Earp and Wild Bill Hickok, Buffalo Bill and George Armstrong Custer. Another group that played a major role in the history of the Old West was the Native American Indians who were basically ignored by the bands at that time. Apart from Neil Young no other artists used Native American imagery as part of their stage persona. The main image Country Rock bands adopted was the one of the Cowboy. This act of putting on the clothes of their forefathers (in some cases great grandfathers) was an act of continuity of young men reclaiming a part of their culture by dressing in the same clothes as their forefathers. By this act of stepping back into the past and adopting the image of the outlaw or cowboy they also reflected the values from that time which to some extent had many parallels to the lifestyle of the rock musician and folk troubadour. Through these actions they not only paid homage to their roots but also identified in a profound way with another lifestyle. There is not a whole lot of difference between saddling a horse with a bedroll and some saddlebags and riding away, than there is packing a rucksack, leaving everything behind you and going 'on the road.' I would propose that Hippies and many of the counter culture were in fact following a sort of 'cowboy code' of shunning convention that back then was represent by railroads and urbanization. In the sixties it was represented by the new age of synthetics coated in plastic. According to Turner the closing of the frontier played a large role in the European settlers adopting a distinctly American identity. His theory was that the people who had lived in the wilderness and fought Indians had evolved into a different breed of man than their European forefathers. According to Turner this has a lot to do with the savagery of Indian fighting. Turner tries to allude to a spiritual kinship with the Native American formed through living in the same terrain and following its rules and traditions among them taking scalps. Through these actions the new breed of American had "outgrown" the European culture and now their roots and culture had become solely American. By the middle of the twentieth century western civilization had experienced two World Wars and some societies like the German one were really sick of the violence and worked towards eradicating it from the society and striving towards a change. Whereas in America and Britain they still cultivated violence and the rule of the gun especially in movies that made a big impression on young men growing up in the post war period. The attitude of young men growing up in the sixties was very much influenced by the movies and TV shows they had been exposed to during the post war decades. This was evident from many of the testimonies of Vietnam veterans who were raised on John Wayne movies. In a darker context these films legalized the use of violence to achieve justice. Many of the GIs in Vietnam say they identified the John Wayne films they had seen as children as a form of instruction on the code of conduct of how men behaved.

The image of the Outlaw and the Cowboy as they were portrayed during the 1950's and early sixties was in many cases portrayed as an outsider and renegade following an unwritten code of a modern day knight helping the underdog or people in need. This image fitted some of the Country Rock bands who supported many of the causes of the counter culture. It is even possible that many rock bands saw themselves as a modern day version of the outlaw. The cover of the album Déjà Vu by CSN&Y at the end of the decade can been seen as the crowning moment of this process where the band steps into a photograph representing the past. In the book "For what it's worth" and in the BBC documentary "Don't be Denied" Neil himself states wryly: "In the old days I used to wear tasselled Jackets, I was young and I guess I thought I was pretty hot." The Rock Stars of the early sixties starting with Elvis Presley were sex symbols idolized by young girls and later came the Beatles and Stones and emerging bands like the Byrds and The Buffalo Springfield. They replaced the gun with a guitar but still followed a very insecure lifestyle with a large element of risk involved. Males that follow these unorthodox lifestyles have somehow always appealed to the opposite sex. It can be seen in the films like 'Shane' and 'The Searchers' where the homesteaders wife is always drawn to the stranger with his rootless existence. She does not want to replace him for her husband but his vulnerability appeals to her feminine side. Her instincts make her want to mother the lost boy and domesticate him. Neil Young had that vulnerability in spades both in the lyrics to his songs and the quiver in his voice and the dark stranger stage persona. Economically like outlaws many of the bands made a hell of a lot of money during the sixties. Neil Young was reputed to be a millionaire at 21.[79] Wealth bought many of them independence and freedom and autonomy to do what they liked artistically. Many of the fans followed the artists on their journey incorporating them into their lives buying their records and attending their concerts. In the Twenty First century nostalgia has become big business in the revival of many sixties bands. The 'Moody Blues' for example who have made nothing of merit in over fifty years can suddenly fill the Albert Hall. Neil Young has never been in this category he has never left the stage or ran out of creative ideas. He has regularly turned out albums and films and various projects like 'Archives'. He is the epitome of the true artist always forging ahead as he follows his muse.

14. Artistic Control and Protest

Neil Young was very much a product of his time and like other artists at that time he started taking artistic control of all the aspects of his work, writing singing and recording his own work. The social political comment in Bob Dylan's lyrics and virtuoso guitar sounds of Jimi Hendrix and Eric Clapton and Cream were pushing the boundaries. By being inspired by each other to do what had never been done before the dominate bands at that time were changing the expectations of the listening public.

In the UK there were always high expectations of anything put out by the Beatles (or the Stones). As Paul Weller said about the Beatles:

"They made you think beyond city walls, you know, of my little town where I come from, they opened me up to the other possibilities in life. They changed the world. I love how creative they were and the

anticipation that with every release they were gonna take you somewhere else. And just the quality of the songs, so many records and so many songs. They were always trying to push forward the boundaries and change people's attitudes as well".

Across the Atlantic the Beatles were also influencing other artists like Brian Wilson who said 'Rubber Soul' was the first Pop music album he heard that seemed to have a whole concept, not just a collection of songs. Albums up to then usually comprised of hit songs and random songs to fill the record. Wilson cites Rubber Soul as an inspiration to making 'Pet Sounds' and the Beatles cite 'Pet Sounds' as an inspiration to 'Sgt. Peppers'. At that time bands collaborated; the Byrds and Beatles exchanged demo tapes and were now focusing more and more on what could be done in the studio and how one could utilize modern technology. The Stones flew to the States on a regular basis to record material. Chess studios were where their idols had recorded. The Stones hoped to acquire a more pure blues sound.

The Beatles used Richard Lester the American director for both their films to give them an American feel.[80] Much of Sgt. Peppers was recorded using multiple four track tape recorders because the multi-track with that many tracks had not been created. By doing this the recording engineers could give the Beatles the effect of a virtual multi track recording studio. The different techniques being used making this album known then as 'reduction mix' or 'bouncing down'. Artists were pushing ahead of the technology available at the time for example during the 'Revolver' sessions to get the desired effect on Lennon's vocals for 'Tomorrow Never Knows' his voice was recorded from the recording console through the Leslie speaker.[81] During 'Revolver' 'automatic double tracking' was also used for the first time.[82]

The Beatles were master craftsmen of their instruments and they wanted to incorporate the recording studio as another dimension in their creative outlet. They dictated to the studio the sound they wanted to create and they recorded it themselves. Previously studios had dictated what was possible in recording sessions and at what time they were open during the day. Now bands had more access and sessions went on through the night. This was evident in the making of Sgt. Pepper where both the recording experience and time it took to record changed the concept about how pop music was made. The listening experience also changed whereas previously you just listened to your favourite tracks. Now you listened to the concept album like a classical symphony from start to finish. This music was so complicated that it could not be performed live. Fans bought it and heard it at home but they would never have the possibility to experience it in a live concert. On top of all this the sophistication of the music and the lyrics made it a tough act for other bands to follow. Once again the Beatles had moved the goalposts and extended the boundaries of what could be achieved in popular music. Through Sgt. Peppers they gave popular music artistic credibility that could not be ignored.

The sophistication of the lyrics on Sgt. Pepper created mental images of a circus act and Victorian Music Hall era mixed with dialogue from a post war Britain with injections of psychedelic jargon. For some reason at that time this sound had a universal appeal and became a proverbial feast of musical creation for the listener. It was released in 1967 just in time for the Summer of Love and dominated the airwaves. In a similar fashion to the way protest songs had a role in influencing what was happening politically and swaying public opinion, the sound of Sgt. Pepper's was turning people on to a new state of consciousness.

Dylan had pointed out on one of his first albums that empty superficial mindless lyrics coming out of the radio were inadequate for the new generation. They needed much more than : "Tell your Ma , tell your Pa, our loves are gonna grow, ooh – wah, ooh- wah"[83] With the expansion of protest songs and progressive experimental music a new kind of social awareness came into being. The Buffalo Springfield established themselves with the Stephen Stills composition "For What it's Worth" a protest song about the riots in LA on Sunset Strip where police used extreme force completely out of proportion with the threat of kids hanging around on the street. Peter Fonda tried to point this out to the

Police and he became the first one arrested in the incident.[84] In a previous incident, the Police beat up Neil Young after arresting him for a driving misdemeanor and knocked one of his teeth out. One member of the Buffalo Springfield had now personally experienced local police violence. "For What it's Worth" encapsulates what was going on in LA and around the United States:

"There's something happening here, what it is aint exactly clear, there's a man with a gun over there, telling me I got to beware"

This song has become a sound bite for the sixties and is often used in contemporary documentaries covering that era. The universal appeal of the song can be found in the Chorus:

"I think we better, Stop people what's that sound? Everybody look what's going down"

It tells us to stop and listen and take note of what we are losing. The civil liberties were being lost in a country that had championed them throughout the world by committing troops to armed conflicts like WW1 and WW2 and the more recent Korean conflict. The longevity of this song was shown when it still struck a poignant note among the audience during the CSN&Y "Freedom of Speech Tour" in 2006.[85] The songs on their first album were a mixture of social comment and love songs. The songs of the second album are more representative of experimental music that was becoming more dominant at the time. During the Summer of Love there was progressive music all around them coming from other LA bands like The Jefferson Airplane with songs like White Rabbit and Lather the airwaves were crammed with vibrant sounds that fed the zeitgeist. These were the sounds that emerged from cars and drifted through shops and parks. People danced to them at parties or lay on beds having an existential experience.

In history Native American tribes had practiced spirituality where they experienced visions through fasting and taking different types of organic hallucinogens like peyote mushrooms and mescaline.

These organic drugs that had once played a major role in Native American cultural rituals were now being adopted by various groups of young people in their quest for enlightenment. Marijuana played a key role in the lifestyle of the sixties. People absorbed the music by smoking a joint and getting high. At that time people who smoked were in tune with each other but by the end of the decade it all turned radically wrong as hard drugs started to take a prominent role in the scene that was happening. Musical artists like David Crosby became casualties. Unlike many of his contemporaries Crosby did not die but he got very strung out and after various trips to rehab eventually ended up in prison. Neil Young dedicated his album "Tonight's the Night" to two people he knew who died from drug overdoses, guitarist Danny Whitten and CSN&Y roadie Bruce Berry. Just as drugs can be said to have enlightened many people in the sixties, they were also responsible for a lot of tragedies.

15. Protest

Alexander Bloom points out music had a very different function in the sixties than it has today:

"Life Magazine might have focused on San Francisco and Haight Ashbury as the capital of "Hippiedom" but these were only its most prominent outcropping. The impact was felt on college campuses, at high schools, in big cities, in small towns, at the movies, and on records – especially on records. Music seemed central to the entire sixties experience, not the narrowly defined cultural role it plays today. Rock bands and folk singers participated in civil rights marches and antiwar rallies. But that is only the surface relationship. The music embodied the same underlying themes, the same sense of creating something new and something better, as did the political and social movements. These all seemed part of the same large endeavor" [86]

Through events like the Monterey Pop Festival, Soul music became affiliated with rock and protest music became more main stream. A protest song like 'Blowing in the Wind' has a universal appeal.

"How many roads must a man walk down, before you can call him a man"? That can be interpreted as a question about life in general. With 'Ohio' Neil Young composed one of the most poignant songs in CSN&Y's catalogue. It is a protest song but it is also a song about the grief and injustice of the murder of the four students whose parents have never received an official apology from the American government. Some of the most prominent protest songs of that era were written by Bob Dylan. He initiated the trend that maybe things could be changed by music (or at least questioned) and many of the spokespeople of the period like the Beatles, Byrds and later CSN&Y would follow his lead. As Alexander Bloom pointed out one of the major factors about the sixties was that the civil rights groups and counter culture interacted with each other. In this way music and protest of the sixties was also expressed by movies and theatre. The whole generation appeared to want change and the courage shown by the counter culture through their music and protests inspired many people working in traditionally conservative areas like Film, Opera and Classical music to ignore some of the restrictions and create what they wanted to express.

One of the main dimensions of that period was that things became less restrictive. It seemed like bastions of culture became less conventional and more experimental. Revolver used chamber music on the song Eleanor Rigby. With Sgt. Pepper the Beatles (with a little help from friend George Martin) took popular music into the realms of serious music. At Woodstock the Who played excerpts from Tommy their new rock opera that they sometimes performed live with the London Symphony Orchestra as backing band. In the early 70's Neil Young went to London to use an orchestra as accompaniment on some of the tracks on Harvest. As an illustration of how big an audience this type of music reached, the commercial success of Harvest made Neil Young the biggest solo artist in the world at that time.

The feeling of liberation that swept through the sixties was contagious Martin Luther King spoke out against the Vietnam War, as the leader of the Black civil rights group which was the most prominent influential group in America he gave support to the antiwar movement. King moved his campaign north to Chicago and the Blank Panther movement was formed. The National Organization for Women (NOW) was formed. Ronald Reagan was elected governor of California his decision to call in the National Guard against students at California University caused a lot of controversy. These developments showed a tendency of what was happening in the society and such action started to have dire consequences. On May 4th 1970 National Guardsmen opened fire on students at Kent State University. They fired 67 shots in 13 seconds killing 4 and leaving 9 wounded one permanently paralyzed.

Neil Young wrote the song Ohio in reaction to this horrific event that stunned America. It was written, recorded and released within a week of the event. The lyrics Four dead in Ohio were very poignant and reference to Nixon and the antiwar sentiment resulted in it being banned some states.[87] All these things became interrelated and they show how the musicians and young people at that time were on the same wavelength. One person wrote on a site they made commemorating the Kent State Massacre 39 years on:

"I am only 28 years old but I remember hearing the songs my mother played as a child and the messages they held." [88]

In 1966 when the Buffalo Springfield formed other things happened that had relevance later: Bill Graham had just started putting on Rock shows at San Francisco's Fillmore Auditorium.

16. Hippies

Hippies and 'Flower Power' played a predominate part of the 'Sixties Revolution' and they are a permanent feature in the event that became known as the 'Summer of Love' in 1967. What exactly is a Hippie? There is no straight answer to that (no pun intended). Originally they are associated with the group that dropped out of the conventional 'College and Career' philosophy and tried to find and alternative way through life, playing music and wearing bright colours. Using drugs and practicing free love were associated with the Hippie lifestyle. They had a set of values that advocated a peaceful existence on earth. The Hippie style and to some extent outlook became a fashion adopted by many young people as a transitory thing. It gave them the opportunity to be free and enjoy their youth while at the same time belonging to something that was considered a legitimate counterpart to conventional lifestyle. It was legitimate in the fact that there was a large following. It should be remembered that Jimi Hendrix was shunned by African Americans for his outrageous dress sense at a time when suits and sunglasses were considered cool among young African Americans. Hendrix was wearing purple velvet flares and Afghan waistcoats with flowered shirts and beads. If he had walked around dressed like that 10 years earlier he would have been locked up as mentally unstable. Now because the hippy movement was becoming a part of the mainstream people had to accept it when it happened in their own little town. That said it was still dangerous to have long hair and wear bright clothes in many States and cities.

Neil Young was beaten up in Canada because of his long hair while trying to hitch hike home after his hearse had broken down at a gig. There was a sincere aspect to the Hippy ideology of wanting the world to change that set them apart from other youth groups like Mods and Rockers who were not really unhappy with the way the world was. They just wanted to be free to wear the clothes they wanted and follow their interests. Whereas Hippies tried to fundamentally change the way they lived, they ate organic food, tried to avoid synthetic products and wanted to bring their children up in a more natural way. They shunned the aggressive consumerism and materialistic lifestyle that was the measure of success in the West. They cared about the planet and the pollution long before it became a trendy political slogan. Many of them as they grew older had to conform and carve out some kind of structured existence to raise their families in. It would be a mistake to think of them as just people who rebelled against their parents when they were young and then started to mirror them as they grew older. In many cases they did not totally abandon their core beliefs.

Many of them retained and outlook and personal values like opposition to war and violence. They filled out tax returns along with the rest of society but the personal commitment to the values of that time. They continued to practice the non-conformity by being political consumers aware of the consequences of production methods concerning the products they buy. Occasionally boycotting products because of the way some countries or multi nationals behave, for example French products after France continued to do nuclear testing. They acknowledged the major role that music played in their lives, in some cases influencing personal decisions about what to do with their lives. At the very least it was the soundtrack to their youth so when they heard one of the songs on the radio today they connect it to their youth. This is apparent with the reissue of many classic sixties albums in special editions, re-mastered with outtakes.

The over fifties age group still figure predominantly in the consumer group this merchandize is produced for. This is somewhat mirrored in the average audience at a Neil Young concert. When I saw him in Berlin in 2006 there was a very mixed bag of old and young people who were making their way through life in various ways but all tuning into the same vibe that I cannot define but it was there.

Neil Young is not a Hippie he is an artist who at various stages of his career has adopted much of the Hippie aura and dress sense. Many Hippies identified with him because of Woodstock and he was a part of their generation experiencing the same events that marked the sixties. No-one can deny that Neil Young's music accompanied by almost schoolboy's lyrics contains a simple beauty that promotes a more harmonious lifestyle; "juggling nickels and dimes". His lyrics conjure up images of sitting on the back porch reflecting or driving down long open highways in pickup trucks being overtaken by Harleys. This supplemented with Neil Young's ever present sense of doubt, a feeling of: I might be happy now but will all this be gone tomorrow? Neil Young acknowledges this natural affinity he has with Hippies in some of his songs like 'Sugar Mountain'.

Not only did music festivals like Monterey, Woodstock, Isle of Wight, Manheim, and Roskilde play a major role in the way music evolved in the sixties. They also showed (with the exception of Altamont) that people could still converge and live together in a large mass with no other intention than digging the vibes. For Hippies smoking marijuana was a communal ritual that to some extent replaced drinking alcohol. People smoked to get mellow and experience the music. Neil Young brings all this together in the song 'Roll another Number' a swansong to the sixties and the hippy era of bygone days when he used to sing Joni Mitchells tender lyrics "We are stardust we are golden and we've got to get ourselves back to the garden." Perhaps an impossible dream to aspire to but people did aspire to it in the sixties. Some of their aspirations especially from designers and artists did trickle down into the society and had an influence on people that we can still feel today. Music changed people's attitudes to things and the way they were living their lives.

In the sixties things opened up, it was no longer necessary to follow preordained lives; you did not have to work in a factory or go down a mine shaft and if you did make the wrong decision the factory and mineshaft was always there to return to. Young people started making conscious decisions to change their lives, like move to London or go on the road. Your life will take a different course and you will have experiences you would not have if you had stayed in a small town working in a factory. The outcome was different for many people and not necessarily always positive. But for some it got them to a place they are quite happy with and they can look back on the years and say "by doing what I did back then, I played a part in the process that got me where I am now".

The Hippie movement did not really have a political agenda but in many cases joined forces and combined with the civil rights protests. The civil rights movement facilitated permanent change in the society in the way people related to each other. People got in touch with their feelings and men were permitted to drop the macho image that had dominated in the West since the end of the war. People could choose how they wanted to live and because of the pill they were not forced to immediately have children. The hitherto confines of dress codes slowly started to disappear. During the sixties, many young families involved in the counter culture dropped out of the materialistic lifestyle and adopted a simpler lifestyle. They lived on farms in collectives, baked their own bread using natural products and made their own clothes. They had to do the daily chores like fetching water and chopping wood. They received a form of spiritual fulfillment from doing this that was associated to the kind of life Snyder was advocating. The Zen Buddhist approach also appealed to a vast segment of the counter culture that was experimenting in mind-expanding drugs and Eastern religions.

'What's happening' was a catchphrase back then. A happening was a spontaneous event where people just gathered and either staged something or just grooved with a joint or bottle of wine sometimes to the accompaniment of a guitar. This is how life once had been in market towns of Europe in the middle ages where people converged to trade and then held festivals, drinking and dancing and celebrating their way of life. There is evidence that there was some kind of revival of these fairs as David Crosby talks about going to Renaissance Fairs outside LA "and I loved everything about them; the girls, the pot, the music, the food, the costumes and the general looseness. People dropped acid all the time. They were the first large gatherings of hippies, even before be-ins."[89] This form of people gathering was also happening in other segments of American society; the Native Americans started reviving their 'Pow Wows'.

The Pow Wow was a tradition that was still within living memory but among some tribes had been discontinued for many years. There were many reasons for this, in some cases it was due to suppression and the 'Americanization' of the Native Americans. Because of this many of the traditions had become obsolete because no-one had passed them on. In many cases where some of the rituals had been forgotten they were able to adopt them again from records made by far sighted

96

anthropologists in the last century. The kinds of activities described by David Crosby were often shunned by straight society who viewed entertainment as an organized activity usually with an admission fee. This was of course the paradox for many of the sixties and seventies bands who started to get rich on record sales and revenues from live performances. On stage these bands espoused freedom but offstage they had become wage slaves like the rest of society, filling out tax forms and conforming to company policies (albeit not all artists did this, some like Neil Young, Dylan, The Stones, Pink Floyd, Led Zeppelin to name a few had made enough money to be truly independent).

Especially in the USA there was a radical departure from the dress code and lifestyle of the fifties where men wore 'Grey Flannel Suits '[90] during the sixties hippies and the various counter culture groups changed the way they dressed. They incorporated many aspects of the old frontier women had long flowing dresses and hair,[91] men wore the jeans and flannel shirts (standard Neil Young attire). In Summer everyone wore sandals and flowery designs, flowers expressed the beautiful essence of nature and the exact opposite of plastic."[92] Some families settled in the mountains in cabins or put up tepees just under the snow line. Here they could be as far away from civilization as possible. These were the areas where rich industrialists purchased retreats that they seldom had time to visit.[93] Grassroots organizations flourished and the fashions and trends created by young people like patched and embroidered jeans started to be mass produced by the establishment thereby erasing much of the individuality. The result was people in general started to dress more casual. In the UK teenagers started to protest about the confinements of their school uniforms and rules concerning hair length not being allowed over the collar.

Attitudes to the environment and eco issues supplement an awareness of what one wore and what one ate. It is necessary to consider all these things together because they were all alternative lifestyles that occurred at the same time thereby working towards and contributing to a collective change. Hippies were a major part of the counter culture of the sixties generation. Their influence was felt not only in their numbers which increased as young people joined them but also in the way they promoted alternative thinking about how we are leading our lives. By voicing concern about the environment and promoting the use of natural products. Hippies indirectly influenced many other groups with these different approaches and lifestyles. One of the major ideals that we had to take care of the planet has only in recent years become a big part of the political agenda. Many people say when reminiscing about the period that there was a sense of unity and solidarity between people and movements like the civil rights groups. This alliance could have come from the fact that in essence everybody really just wants the right to exist and practice their own way of life.

The counter culture realized that what the civil rights movements were fighting for was an integral part of everyone's right. Another aspect was the Hippies were a minority without the legal justification that ethnic and religious groups had. Hippies were in a vulnerable situation on the periphery of a society controlled by people with very conservative attitudes. Opposition to the Vietnam War and the draft was one of the aspects that united the counter culture with the mainstream. Especially after Mylai, it became a common struggle.

Sometimes the establishment hit 'a warp' and inadvertently supported them. When research showed that marijuana was less harmful to the body than alcohol or Harvard University Professor, Timothy Leary, encouraging young people to "turn on, tune in and drop out".

Tremors went through the society when celebrities like the Beatles and others admitted to using recreational drugs.[94] Dr. Leary could never have achieved what he did on such a scale if there was not already a tendency that society was moving in that direction. He put his career on the line as a reputable Harvard professor and spoke out for what he believed was right at the time to the universal soundtrack of "The Times they are a Changing." Of all the patriots who should be the most patriotic if not the leaders? Yet it is well documented that not one member of congress had a son serving in Vietnam. The counter culture exposed the hypocrisy in the system and pointed at the failings of imperialism. On humanistic grounds at the very least we in the West did not have the right to govern over and suppress civil liberties of third world countries on the other side of the planet, exploiting their natural resources and labour costs. The Hippie movement was the most radical of the counter culture movement in many regards. They promoted and encouraged a lifestyle to such an extent that the sixties would not have been the sixties without the Hippies. They are one of the predominate factors in the collective imagination, when recalling that period. Without the Hippie dimension shaking things up during the sixties life would definitely have been a lot more dogmatic.

Equality and Civil Rights would have been achieved but the transition would have been much less colourful and spiritually we would have vastly poorer than we are today. There would have been no Summer of Love and what happened in California at that time was defiantly a high water mark in the whole evolution that took place. No-one associated with that time can belittle the sincerity of the Hippie movement and its belief in passive resistance. Flower Power and the beauty of nature combined with meditation and Eastern Religions vastly helped to change the Western outlook. Neil Young knew that and he lamented it in some of his songs. Many of his fans could recognize the message and related it to the passing of the era in the same way that he did. These songs were very real to anyone who had been through that period and can look back on it with some affection. The world would never be the same again.

17. Record Covers

For some people their record collection from the sixties is very special to them. Even though they might have renewed it with the CD versions of the old classics, they still have not ditched the vinyl. This could be because they encapsulate periods in their lives that they remember when they play them. Some of the cover art from the period have become iconic and are easy to recognize. The Beatles LP cover for Revolver for example was drawn by Klaus Voorman and is a classic cover. Some of the others like Sgt. Peppers by Peter Blake are considered real works of art. The Stones used Andy Warhol for a cover and for their logo. A cover like Déjà Vu you could hang on the wall. In many cases the record sleeves were not just packaging they were also designed to make a statement or reflect a style and image the band wanted to project. Many portrayed the group like a pin up for the fans. The Beatles White Album was a form of modern art by having nothing on it at all except an impression of the band's name supplemented by a collection of individual portraits of the band inside. The whole genre of promoting bands and their records and concerts through sleeves, posters, and flyers were extremely creative as can be seen by the Fillmore posters and other venues where bands like Buffalo Springfield , Jefferson Airplane, The Grateful Dead and Country Joe and the Fish played. The genre of promoting the music varied just as the style of the music varied.

Many Blue Note Jazz covers really capture the feeling of the fifties just as Psychedelic Rock covers represent the 60's in a different way to say Tamla Motown's chart Busters volume 5 where the sleeve looked like it was made out of tin foil. This volume of greatest hits that would usually be considered an unlikely candidate found its way into many record collections. Tamla Motown was doing to working class African Americans what Mersey Beat was doing to their white English working class counterparts. Putting them in suits and presenting them to a wider audience. The connection was not only visual, Rock music as the Beatles and others pointed out came from the blues where soul music also originated so there is a logical affiliation. This could be seen at Monterey Pop festival featuring Otis Redding here Soul music was given the opportunity to reach a wider audience.

Neil Young did some of his early recording sessions with the Mynah Birds at Tamala Motown's studio in Detroit. Motown did to soul music what Nashville did to Country and Western they created a distinctive sound of high quality. Like Neil Young said if you were unable to create a sound Motown had session men that could recreate the exact sound required. That's how all the bands on that label managed to sound so polished and easily recognizable. Many record collections tended to be an assortment of different tastes and styles of music. Hendrix had some Bob Dylan and a copy of Gustav Holt's Planets along with Bonzo Dog Doo Dah Band in his collection when he died. People would hear something at a friend's house, like it and buy the record. I have sometimes seen a record in a friend's collection that appears to be totally out of place and when I ask about it, they reply something like "Oh, that's just something we bought on holiday in London, we had such a good time and it was always on the radio".[95] This shows how records become private reference points that people relate to in a very personal way. This social interaction between radio and records were vital in the sixties to exposing the music to the populace. To do this DJ's got 'advanced promotional copies from the record companies that they could play to fans weeks in advance. There were no downloads or internet at that time. They came directly from the manufacturers with a plain white label stamped 'PROMOTIONAL COPY NOT FOR SALE.' These pre-issues sometimes created such a demand that the records went straight into the charts when they were released.

18. Sgt. Pepper contra John Wesley Harding

Bob Dylan's album John Wesley Harding was released later in the same year as Sgt. Peppers 1967. For this album, Dylan reached back to the same period in his country's history as the Beatles had done. Where the Beatles chose a Victorian style military band from the heyday of the British Empire, Dylan chose the Texas gunfighter from the 1860s known as John Wesley Harding who was reputed to have shot around 40 men. On the cover Of John Wesley Harding there are three relatively unknown people who could easily be mistaken for Native Americans but are in fact real Indian musicians from India.

The Beatles choosing a military band from around this time was defiantly not a pacifist statement. Every regiment at that time would have had a band that played on parades and military tattoos. Most children growing up in the 1950's would have experienced the pageantry of military tattoos and John Lennon is reputed to have attended some while on holiday in Scotland. Also noticeable is that Ringo bears the rank of sergeant on the cover. Besides being the backbone of the British Army it was the highest rank that a working class person could normally hope to achieve in the Victorian era. They are surrounded by their heroes and people they admired the only one strongly objected to by the record management was Gandhi who was deleted from the collage. Mae West had objected saying *"What would I be doing in a lonely hearts club"* but after the Beatles wrote her individual letters pleading their case she consented.

Dylan chose a gunfighter hero of the Old West; he challenged the Beatles extravagance stylistically and musically. Sgt. Pepper was the first real "studio album" it had taken six months in the studio to record and because of its complexity made it extremely difficult to perform live. The 12 songs on John Wesley Harding were done in three sessions totaling 12 hours. The style was Nashville country folk rock suitable for live performance. The artist Peter Blake designed the cover of Sgt. Pepper the life size collage took two weeks to create. The cover for Dylan's LP is in black and white it is very modest and simple in construction. Bob Dylan's manager, Albert Grossman lived next door to Dylan and the picture was taken in his garden. Grossman had some musicians from India staying with him and two of them are on the cover together with his gardener. They used two photographers for the shoot one used a Polaroid so Dylan could chose the one he wanted straightaway. This example together with the one of how 'Easy Rider' was made shows there was no economic formula; projects that came from both ends of the economic spectrum could achieve commercial success. It was a mixture of creative ideas, luck and the commitment of the artist to their work that the fans seemed to recognize and support. These albums clearly illustrate the diversity of popular music from that period. The interesting thing is how they both reached into the same period of history in their respective countries. Neil Young was still up and coming at this time and will have been influenced by both these groundbreaking albums.

Neil Young is often singled out as Bob Dylan's only contemporary when looking at artists from the sixties and their artistic output. Even though Neil Young is considerably younger than Bob Dylan or the Beatles they have similar track records (no pun intended). None of them has really ever given in to commercial pressure. They have all experienced periods in their careers of legal disputes with record companies and bad reviews from critics about their music. But they always came back supported by the loyalty of their fans and their own artistic innovation. The lesson learned in the sixties was that: 'there is no formula'.

Many things came as a complete surprise and were not anticipated at all by the industry. For example the dominant role played by popular music, the popularity of low budget films with Rock soundtracks, the massive attendance of the Woodstock music festival. These things happened because people with a vision initiated them. Albums like John Wesley Harding, Pet Sounds and Sergeant Peppers were markers set down by the artists to lead the way forward. Just as they had done with Blonde on Blonde and Revolver, Dylan and the Beatles were at the top of their profession and what they put out was seen as the benchmark of quality that other bands had to strive to achieve.

19. Ready Steady Go and Top of the Pops

The TV shows 'Ready Steady Go' (ITV, 1966 – 68) and 'Top of the Pops' (BBC 1967 – 2006) was for many young people across the UK during the sixties the only visual source of live music acts that people had. In the early sixties if you lived outside London where the major Rock venues were you had government controlled BBC radio playing 45 minutes a day of playing rock music (at the time this kind of music was considered immoral and could corrupt young people). Some lucky ones could pick up AFN,[96] and Luxemburg or the Pirate stations Caroline and Radio London. [97] Unless you lived in a University town or your Technical College had a good students union organizing concerts you were dependent on the radio and the local record store where they stocked the latest singles and LPs. These shops were decorated with posters and flyers publicizing artists of record companies like Liberty, Atlantic, EMI and Island. These labels also released cheap LPs called samplers that were compellations of songs from bands on that label. Some of the notable ones were 'Gutbucket' and 'Son of Gutbucket' on the Liberty label or 'Nice Enough to Eat' on the Island. The Atlantic label released the 'Age of Atlantic' in 1970 and this sampler cost 99 pence. It featured Buffalo Springfield's 'Broken Arrow' and was for many Brits their first exposure to Buffalo Springfield. The sampler also contained tracks by Iron Butterfly, Vanilla Fudge, MC5, Delaney and Bonnie, Dr. John, Allman Brothers Band, Cold Blood, Dada and the emerging giant Led Zeppelin's "Communication Breakdown" and 'Whole Lotta Love' which ensured reasonable record sales in the UK.

Top of the Pops enjoyed immense popularity during the sixties and featured a female dance troop called 'Pans People' who danced to some of the most popular tunes and songs at that time. They often danced to American songs where the bands were not available to perform live in the TV studio. Hendrix managed to perform on both shows having started his career in the UK. "The Good the Bad and the Ugly" Enrico Morricone's composition to the last film in Serge Leone's famous 'Dollar trilogy', that topped the UK charts in 1966.

As a 12 year old boy I remember vividly watching Pans People doing their dance routine clad in ponchos, cowboy hats and knee high boots. Dancing to the instantly recognizable ominous rhythmic whistling and chanting. Ruth Pearson one of Pans People recalls when asked if there were any particular songs she did not like: "Many [laughs]. Some songs and concepts suited different people and some I couldn't stand, but then that was the challenge as the song. But it all went hand in hand with the song. Like 'The Good, The Bad And The Ugly', and 'Tie A Yellow Ribbon Round The Old Oak Tree'. There was quite a lot of those. The music, the clothes and the dances all made some of it a bit... bleurgh!" She was obviously not a fan of Spaghetti Westerns. Designers like Mary Quant in England who launched the mini skirt and were enhancing the female image much to the consternation of the older generation. Designers like her were giving real alternatives to female fashion that up to that point had been literally a choice between brown shoes or black shoes to wear with long pleated dresses or skirts. Women did not wear jeans in Europe during the early sixties. The modern designs inspired by Mary Quant with miniskirts and colourful boots and scarves became the staple of Pans People's wardrobe. Some people considered the Pan's People's minimalistic dress code very improper at the time. To this Ruth Pearson replies:

"You have to remember that those clothes were pretty much the style of the time. We were only wearing what young people were wearing. I suppose some people were tut-tutting about it but that's always happened over the years, and still happens now. I'm sure I got my fair share of tutting but in general my parents dealt with it very well." [98]

I use this example with Pans People because for many young people in the UK seeing them perform on Top of the Pops was one of the highlights of the week. Their style was very representative of the 'Swinging London' image being projected at the time and as Ruth Pearson says they were wearing what young people were wearing. This was true on both sides of the Atlantic what bands were wearing at the time was reflective of and inspiring youth fashion. This is evident in some of the Rustie's statements and clothes descriptions.

Top of the Pops was without doubt the main weekly music program on TV in the UK. I recall seeing Neil Young on the show in 1972[99] he appeared performing "Heart of Gold" the only number one single in his long career.[100] Among the best 500 songs of all time Rolling Stone magazine rated the song number 297. Neil Young sits onstage dressed as a 'Mountain man' with his long hair falling over his face as he sings. There he sat alone with an acoustic guitar and a harmonica and a dress code that was in stark contrast to the 'Glam Rock' fashion that was prevailing in the UK at that time. Although he looked like he had just finished chopping wood, they were in fact his stage clothes. As his artist friend James Mazzeo states "Neil only wore his old patched jeans when performing" (see cover of After the Goldrush). During this televised performance he had what looked like a 'joint' in his harmonica holder and at the end of the song he takes a toke and flashes one of those 'wickedest of grins,'[101] at the camera. He might not have looked like much at the time but he was a member of Crosby Stills Nash and Young the only American group to approach the popularity of the Beatles and with Harvest Neil Young became a superstar in his own right. The people loved his music and the sound of this solo album dominated the airways. Led Zeppelin front man Robert Plant caught Neil's performance in the states and is quoted as saying "what Neil Young did on the guitar brought tears to my eyes". Many of Led Zepplins songs like 'Goin to California'[102] are clearly inspired by Neil Young and the other artists of the Canyon.

I have not been able to trace the Neil Young appearance on Top of the Pops and it is quite possible it was lost when the BBC introduced a policy in the 1970's of 'junking' old programs.[103] This is not only a tragedy because we have lost Neil Young's stage act but also because the dress and style of the audiences gave a clear picture of the diversity in the society at that time and the atmosphere associated with such events.

20. The History: Closing of the Frontier 1890

One of the most significant events in American history after the American Civil War was the closing of the frontier. The army had made America safe for expansion by brutally putting down the Native Americans and driving them from their homelands. At the same time hunters and settlers destroyed the Buffalo herds to make way for railroads and cattle. One of the last prominent Native American leaders still fighting was Geronimo. He was the chief of the Chiricahua Apache and continued protecting the Apache way of life by fleeing over the Mexican border and organizing guerrilla actions against the American government from there. Geronimo finally surrendered in Sept 1886 and was taken to a military prison in Florida. With the Wounded Knee massacre[104] in 1890 the frontier was officially closed. This was the last military action against Native Americans living freely outside a reservation.

In 1905 Geronimo and other Native American chiefs took part in President Theodore Wilson's inauguration parade. In 1901 Queen Victoria died and Geronimo eventually died in captivity in 1909.[105] These two events marked the symbolic closing of eras on both sides of the Atlantic. In America the frontier closed completing the colonization of America. In Great Britain the curtain fell on the Victorian age, where the British Empire had been the most dominant force on the planet. If we look at these historical points they illustrate how close people were in the mid-sixties to these events. People born when Geronimo and Queen Victoria died were only in their sixties in the 1960's. When AIM was formed in the 1968 there were still people alive who had experienced some of these events. In less than a decade after Geronimo's death, 12000 Native Americans fought for the United States in WW1 when it joined the conflict in 1917.[106] Some Native Americans were given citizenship in recognition of their contribution to the fighting in WW1. This action helped a common identity to form by building on the tradition of Indian scouts that served in the US forces during the previous century. In the same token, colonial forces of the British and French Empires served in millions fighting against the Germans on the Western Front.

For many of them it was a stunning first-hand experience of European culture where they experienced for the first time whites that were not only poor but doing manual labour! This had a profound effect on them and contributed to the process that would eventually lead some of their countries to independence. The African Americans had another experience in a different context. They were treated as equals by the French receiving decorations for bravery and allowed to march in victory parades. Only to be segregated and discriminated against when they returned home to the United States. From this experience in Europe African Americans could see that the way they were forced to live in America and serve in a segregated military was profoundly wrong. This practice continued in the US military throughout world war two and was finally abolished in 1946.

There was a synchronization and synthology in many of the events and beliefs that emerged or re-emerged in the sixties. There was a worldwide support of the anti-war and civil rights movements. People had experienced the extremes of WW2 and now they were bombarded with images of distraught Vietnamese civilians and wounded GI's. This provoked protest: Why was this necessary? When was it going to stop? While there was all this media focus against violence, there was a parallel movement in the entertainment industry focusing on the same violent period towards the end of the 19th century. There appeared to be a revival in the UK and the USA of two historical periods that went back the same amount of years but had vastly different outcomes. In the USA the films were about the Indian wars and frontier life. In the UK films were based on major events in the Empire, 'Waterloo,' 'Charge of the Light Brigade' and 'Zulu' were immensely popular and helped to bring the 'Military Look' into vogue. In both instances clothes from that era were used by the Rock Bands in their respective countries. With the exception of Hendrix who sported a British military jacket wrongly referred to as a Hussars jacket.[107] One of the noticeable differences was that the Americans took their history up to revival whereas the British to some extent glorified theirs.

Through the 'Counterculture Westerns from the mid-sixties there emerged the 'New Cult of the Indian' giving the Native Americans and their culture a key role in the history and ethnography of the United States "This renewed interest coincided with (and was energized by) the renewal of Native American political movements whose emergence on the national scene was signaled by the organization of the American Indian Movement AIM formed in 1968 and the publication of Vine Deloria's 'Custer Died for Your Sins' in 1969.[108] One of the results of this revival was that it assisted and supported the cause of the Native Americans and without doubt helped to change their situation drastically and the major reforms they achieved at the time led to self-autonomy in the Native American communities that we see today.

21. Buffalo Bill

Buffalo Bill was the first American showman to leave America with a Wild West Show and achieve international acclaim. In 1887 he left America for England with his company of 200 men, women and children.[109] Almost a 100 Indians among them many veterans of famous frontier battles like the Little Big Horn. Below decks 200 animals including 180 horses and 18 Buffalo along with 300 saddles hundreds of guns and an arsenal of ammunition. Twelve covered wagons and the Deadwood stagecoach. These figures show just how big this company was. The audiences would experience Indians hunting Buffalo and attacking wagon trains with many displays of marksmanship using live ammunition. Annie Oakley shot the cigarette out of the Kaisers mouth at one performance.[110]

With his performances Bill gave audiences in Europe and America a final chance to experience the Old West. Bill had Major Burke as a PR manager "who must rank as one of the greatest PR men in history."[111] Not only did he build up the myth of Buffalo Bill but promoted the shows with colourful poster depicting 'Frontier ' scenes of Cowboys, Scouts and Indians. Western paraphernalia like Wooden Tomahawks, Books, Post-Cards, Dime novels and programs where sold at all the shows.[112] Further evidence how the Native Americans history was interrelated can be seen when some Indian Chiefs met Queen Victoria after they performed in Buffalo Bill`s Wild West show at her Golden Jubilee in 1887. Though some of them had taken part in the Battle of the Little Big Horn they called her their "*White Mother*" and were impressed at her trust in meeting them alone and not accompanied by her warriors!

Buffalo Bill had been a Chief Scout for the Army and was a friend of Wild Bill Hickok and Custer and as I will explain later played a major role in Frontier History.[113] When the frontier closed, the Indians were sent to live on reservations. These reservations could be described as open prisons inside marked areas. In the beginning they were administered by army forts. Today many Native Americans have settled in towns and cities, but a large percentage of them continue to live on the reservations that were originally allocated to them by the American government when the frontier closed. It has been estimated that the European Americans in their colonization of the United States wiped out around eight million Native Americans. There is an on-going debate on the numbers killed ranging from two to fifteen million and the use of the term genocide or democide. This is an important aspect of American history because it acknowledges that the war the Native Americans fought was to protect their way of life. So many of them died in a war they eventually lost. But without a doubt this event was a major contribution to the American experience. It also puts the Native American Civil Rights movement that emerged in the sixties into perspective. Along with the extraordinary events that happened after the frontier closed with reservations and forced integration through boarding schools and banning of rituals and culture.

Native Americans were not allowed to celebrate events that were important to them and in the twentieth century Wild West Shows found recruiting Native Americans difficult because of enforced government restrictions. All these events contributed to the final integration into the society and consciousness of the American people in the 20th century. During the 19th century the Native Americans like Sitting Bull and Lone Wolf who had been fighting the white man now toured with Buffalo Bill and experienced European culture first-hand. Meeting heads of state and being a part of spreading American history and culture.

"The ultimate financial failure of Buffalo Bill's Wild West should not obscure its unparalleled success as a myth making enterprise. From 1885 to 1905 it was the most important commercial vehicle for fabrication and transmission of the myth of frontier. The period of its European triumph coincided with the period of massive immigration to America. As many immigrants testified, the Wild West was the source of some of their most vivid images and expectations of the new land."[114]

This clearly shows the importance of the image of the Old West that Bill promoted. He had many friends among the Native Americans and considered Sitting Bull his old adversary to be his friend. They were both remnants of a bygone era and carried with them parallel memories of life on the plains. Even though they saw that life from very different standpoints many whites mourned to see that life disappear as Fredric Sackrider Remington wrote in 1905:

"I knew the railroad was coming. I saw men already swarming into the land. I knew the derby hat, the smoking chimneys, the cord binder and the 30 day note were upon us in a restless urge. I knew the wild riders and the vacant land were about to vanish forever, and the more I considered the subject, the bigger the forever loomed."

When Buffalo Bill spoke to the press in Europe about those days he defended the Native Americans telling reporters, *"In nine cases out of ten when there is trouble between the white man and Indians, it will be found that the white man is responsible for the dispute for breaking faith with them."* More poignantly concerning Custer he told the press,

" The defeat of Custer was not a massacre. The Indians were being pursued by skilled fighters with orders to kill. They had their wives and little ones to protect, and they were fighting for their existence."[115]

These statements were very progressive for the time considering the fact that the official revision of the role of the Native American in American history first started seventy years later in Life Magazine. The July 2nd 1971 edition had two portraits of Native Americans on the cover under the title *'Our Indian Heritage,'*[116] there was a special section complete with a revisionist account of the Indian wars which emphasized white peoples responsibility and celebrated leaders like Crazy Horse as: *Great Men not Savages.*[117] For the whole cast of the Wild West Show there were many experiences during their European tour that gave them reason to be proud the be American. In some cases their reactions that would normally be viewed as breach of protocol probably added to the excitement of the experience to the audience.

At Queen Victoria's jubilee for example as the cast marched in, the American flag was waved. With the statement that it was an 'emblem of peace and friendship to all in the world.'

"Her majesty rose from her seat and bowed deeply and impressively towards the banner. The whole court party rose, the ladies bowed and the generals present saluted, and the English noblemen took off their hats. Then – we couldn't help it – there arose such a genuine heart stirring American yell from our company as seemed to shake the sky." [118]

This shows the high status of Buffalo Bill and his Wild West Show among European dignitaries.. This was truly a seminal event as it was the first time since the American Declaration of independence that a British sovereign saluted the American flag. This would increase the prestige and status given to Buffalo Bill back in America. For the Native Americans present it must have been a strange and possibly moving moment as they are being collectively honoured in something that they must have had difficulty being wholeheartedly a part of. Even though they had always been well treated by Buffalo Bill they were representing the losing side and in a way celebrating in the performances the loss of the Native American way of life. Despite this America was their country and that is where their loyalty remained. Afterwards they spoke with great respect for Queen Victoria calling her their 'White Mother' and now she was honouring them as a part of the American community.[119]

At the World's Fair held in Chicago in 1893, America had tried to play down the frontier image and promote their advancement in technology as an industrial nation. Nevertheless, the public showed their preference by selling out Buffalo Bills shows that were situated close to the exhibition. Frederick Turner gave his thesis on the closing of the frontier at the exhibition. Showing that aspect of American life was still prominent in people's minds. This attraction for the nature and frontier was brought to the surface again in people's consciousness through the films and music of the sixties. Neil Young reached into this period of History on a professional level when he named his band "Crazy Horse" and on a personal level when he named one of the Buffalo from his herd 'Cody'. This animal was used in the film 'Dancing with Wolves' and is reputed to be very good at following instructions. At one point Neil Young always performed with a wooden 'Cigar Store Indian' with him onstage. He used the term Broken Arrow for the title of a song, the name of his recording studio and the ranch that he lives on. After the Buffalo Springfield period, the name Neil Young is still associated with these Native American terms. They are repeated in books and articles until they form familiar associations in our minds. This association with the name Crazy Horse has resulted in our acceptance of Neil Young's name in connection with the visual Native American imagery he used on record covers, posters other merchandize like T-shirts with Native American images. In that sense, there are similarities with Buffalo Bill's 'Wild West Show'. Wild West regalia used by the American Country Rock bands during the mid-sixties and into the seventies as well as being an act of reclaiming their cultural heritage. It also promoted their products and affiliated them to the genre of country rock music. More importantly, it placed them squarely as an American phenomenon.

Most of the Country Rock bands in LA, Buffalo Springfield included, opted for the Western look of the cowboy, dressing up in Calvary uniforms and cowboy clothes for promotional photo shoots.[120] The bands came predominately from LA and California. Buffalo Springfield and the Byrds spearheaded the movement followed by The New Riders of the Purple Sage, Don Nix, Gary Puckett and the Union Gap and later the Eagles. The Western style of clothing they used appeared more authentic and became a dress code for the counter culture. Not just Hippies but young people in general wore jeans and tasselled jackets with waistcoats and cowboy boots or moccasins. The only thing that would place them in the 2oth century were the sunglasses and the watches. David Crosby's father received an Oscar for his work as cinematographer on the classic Western 'High Noon' so one can assume that he knew what a Western was while growing up. He often wore cowboy hats and tasselled jackets while performing with the Byrds and he continued using this image when he joined CSN. [121]

22. Western Movies.

The influence of westerns on males growing up in the United States in the 50's was one of the most dominating factors in their lives. Martin Scorsese says of westerns in an interview reviewing a Budd Boetticher DVD collection "it's about who we are and where we come from".[122] The Western is the American history and cultural roots, no-one can dispute that. The stereotype of the cowboy is someone single minded and fiercely independent as seen in characters like Shane. This quality was admired in people who see the role of maverick as a positive image. In American popular culture the guy who goes against the grain and succeeds become popular like the test pilot Chuck Jaeger. The analogy of the open skies and the open prairies is appropriate just as the parallels between the sky being the new frontier in the middle of the twentieth century and the original American Western Frontier, neither of them suitable for the faint hearted.

The influence of cowboy movies on young children and especially boys growing up in the 50's and 60's is immeasurable. Throughout the Western World children played Cowboys and Indians and watched weekly programs like 'Wagon Train', 'Rawhide', 'The Lone Ranger' and 'Gunsmoke' these along with black and white westerns became staple diet for many young children growing up . Cowboy outfits, guns, bows and arrows were available in toy stores everywhere. I have vivid recollections of being perched in suspense watching a lone pony express rider trying to outrun an Indian war party or Ben Johnson galloping away from a War Party and jumping his horse over a ravine to escape (all ripping stuff). John Fords main actor might have been John Wayne but many young boys aspired to be the character of sergeant Tyree depreciatingly played by the actor Ben Johnson in 'She Wore a Yellow Ribbon.' He was always the guy who got out of tight spots and often excelled his officers in his knowledge of Indian customs and tactics. On the DVD of extra material released with John Ford's 'The Searchers' an interview with Ben Johnson shows that time has not faded him, he still has some of the depreciating mannerisms that his characters had in the early John Ford films. Even as an older man in the interview he still retains that youthful boyish charm that won him a place in people's hearts. His acting in all those Westerns sometimes portrayed an innocent immature outlook on life. That one could say is a soft underbelly of the rugged cowboy exterior of ruthless single-mindedness that is necessary when facing up to something unpleasant. These are some of the key elements in the cowboy's foundations that give him an aura of inner contentment. The kind of person who takes all the good things and bad things that life throws at him in his stride. Being English I could not personally appreciate Westerns as cultural roots in the way Scorsese categorizes them for Americans (This is who we are; this is where we come from.) I enjoyed them immensely; I guess part of the attraction to young boys is you can master the rudimental skills quite easily, riding an imaginary horse over urban wasteland and shooting a toy gun. This was much like what McCartney said in an early interview about emerging bands in the UK, "you did not need any kind of qualifications to be in a band."[123] Despite the physical and ideological distance between America and most of the Western World after WW2 the genre of the American Western films helped to indoctrinate young boys into the 'American Way.' They gave young boys role models and values in connection with male identity and what they thought male behavior should be in relationship to the treatment of indigenous people, women and the use of violence to solve problems. There was a male code in the Western that Clint Eastwood has always utilized in his Westerns that even for the bad guy there was a clear definition of right and wrong. A positive element that is noticeable in the pre-1960 Westerns is the amount of singing going on, in theme tunes and round the camp fire or in saloon bar scenes. The male camaraderie and songs were an intricate part of these early black and white films. The image of a cowboy riding across the prairie strumming a guitar could be a powerful image on an impressionable young man. Neil Young has revealed that he enjoyed watching old cowboy movies as a kid but SF was really the main attraction.

"What kind of movies did you see and love as a boy? Japanese horror and Science fiction movies-Invaders from Mars and stuff like that. I loved the fantasy. I also liked old Westerns, but I really liked the interplanetary stuff the best. It takes me away. I'm very uneducated. I used to think Abbott and Costello were funny. I loved Jerry Lewis movies. I thought they were fine art. But I also like long shots and ambience of the early Federico Fellini and Jean-Luc Godard pictures." [124]

I have been considering the Western film genre to see what kind of film Neil Young might have seen as a boy growing up in Canada. To say this is a vast area is a mega understatement it would probably take about four years to get through all the Gene Autry and Roy Rodgers and other B movies. (It is however advisable to check out Budd Boetticher whose B Westerns were an inspiration to Clint Eastwood, Martin Scorsese and other directors).Then it would take another four years of viewing to get through the regular matinees then if there was any time left you could check out the abundance of Western series made for TV.

For this reason I have narrowed down the field by focusing only on what has become known as John Ford's 'Calvary Trilogy' plus 'The Searchers' all of which are now considered classic Westerns. 'Fort Apache' was made in 1948 followed by 'She wore a Yellow Ribbon' in 1949. The last one of the trilogy was 'Rio Grande' made 1950. 'The Searchers' was made in 1956,[125] it is said that Ford made the Searchers and later Cheyenne Autumn to try and make a amends for his negative portrayal of Native Americans in his previous films. The Searchers can in some respects be seen as a forerunner of the revisionist Westerns that came in the sixties. That could be part of the reason it was so badly received when it came out, it was too far ahead of its time. It now holds the prestigious position of the best Western ever made. All the films in Fords Cavalry trilogy are fine examples of Westerns from their respective periods and although one should keep in mind they were made for entertainment not historical documentation there is evidence that John Ford knew his history and was an avid enthusiast of old American folk music and Country and Western songs. His intricate knowledge is evident in the skillful way he incorporates music in his films to compliment the fantastic scenery around Monument Valley creating an ambience of the Old West. Many of the areas where he filmed were not even connected by roads at that time. Many of the Native American extras he used in the scenes were born in the era of the closing of the frontier. As they were growing up their ancestor's way of life was going through its death throes. They would still go hunting on the prairies that would give them a natural affinity to rifles and listen to tales of how life used to be but the door on their lifestyle was closing. What Ford is able to give us is a good imitation of how life probably was and because he did it at a time when much of the natural areas had not been developed we are able to experience them in a convincing way. Without doubt his use of Native American actors contributes immensely to giving the Calvary Trilogy that is shot in black and white a distinct feeling of authenticity.

In 1913 when moving pictures were in their infancy Buffalo Bill had the foresight to make a film documenting historical events before they faded from living memory. The idea was to capture the 27 key events that he considered critical to the American experience of the conflict with the Native Americans and the closing of the frontier. It was originally titled "The Last Indian Wars" and shortened to "The Indian Wars". Filming began under the direction of Theodore Wharton at the Pine Ridge Indian reservation on October 11th 1913 after three weeks rehearsals and ended 17 days later.[126] The secretary of War Lindley M. Garrison permitted troops from the 12th Calvary based at Fort Robinson Nebraska to participate in the film alongside Native American counterparts and some of Buffalo Bills "Show Indians." General Miles and Native Americans who had participated in events were used as advisors. The scenes were sometimes shot at the original locations using some of the original participants. Bill Cody wanted the events like Wounded Knee to be historically correct showing the slaughter of innocent women and children but General Miles balked at this saying that it would be against public interest. It was a delicate subject and cause of some disputes between the Native Americans and film makers who played down Indian success and prowess in battle and disguised massacres against women and children as fair fights against worriers. The film was not a commercial success and unfortunately has been lost to prosperity, only a few scenes from the eight reel epic remain.[127]

Buffalo Bill filmed "The Indian Wars" 25 years after the events took place and around 25 years after Buffalo Bill made his film John Ford started to film his interpretation of the conflicts along the frontier. We are left with his sometimes spectacular films as a primary source. These can also come in handy if you are studying Country and Western music as he used the original renowned group The Sons of the Pioneers in some of his films. John Ford has many negative points in his portrayal of the Native American in his early films. He was however a great film director who also knew some of the participants of some of the historical events. For example in 'My Darling Clementine' he restaged the Gunfight at OK Corral and because he had known Wyatt Earp he claimed it to be historically authentic. Ford had great skill as a storyteller and goes into fine details about characters' lives and relationships. In the trilogy many of the characters like Trooper Tyree continue through the series getting older and rising in rank to Sergeant.

The trilogy was not made as such but has become known among film buffs as 'John Fords Calvary Trilogy.' One cannot judge them by the norms we have today and they should be viewed as intelligently made popular entertainment from that period. Viewing them today it is easy to imagine the impression they would have made on adolescent young boys and young Native Americans.

Ford Apache is the first of the trilogy was made in 1948 only two years after the end of WWII. The film shows vivid scenes of violence and sacrifice so soon after the end of a war that became the ultimate symbol of violence and sacrifice in the twentieth century. Henry Fonda plays an 'Old School' Commanding Officer who demands discipline and despises the Indians who defy the United States government. He is willing to sacrifice himself and his troops to try to force Cochise into submission. The film clearly shows how the 'white man' unscrupulously deceives the Indian. The commanding officer Colonel Owen Thursday, played by Henry Fonda sends John Wayne to Mexico to negotiate with Cochise knowing Cochise will trust him. John Wayne returns successful and the Colonel Thursday wants to set a trap for Cochise and his warriors which would result in John Wayne breaking his word. Against advice from John Wayne Colonel Thursday proceeded to attack Cochise who is in a heavily defended fortified position. This results in his group of Calvary being wiped out. John Wayne is left in command of the reserves and as he awaits the imminent onslaught, Cochise rides up and symbolically gives John Wayne the captured Calvary flag. This portrays the Indian to be more even handed and honorable than the white man. A theme that was the basis of most of the 'Counter Culture Westerns' released in the sixties.[128] A feeling of mutual respect between Wayne and Cochise closes the picture. However by portraying the adversary as superior you enhance your own achievements when you eventually defeat them in battle. This might not have been Ford's motivation at that time as the film ends with the Native Americans undefeated and honorable. The role of the Native Americans is not the main focus of the movie. The main focus is more on the commanding officer Own Thursday and his daughter and their relationship to the members of the command of Fort Apache. There is also the critical interpretation given by the commanding officer Lieutenant Colonel Owen Thursday that the treatment of the Native Americans was necessary in a Machiavellian sense that the end justified the means. It was necessary to behave in this manner to create the United States. Some people had to be cold and brutal like the Henry Fonda character Owen Thursday in Fort Apache and the John Wayne's character Ethan in The Searchers. We don't like to openly associate with them and we do not in any means condone their conduct. But we live with the results and reap the benefits of their actions, although we naturally condemn the methods used to gain them. War is war and all the terrible things that are done in the name of justice, to make sure your side wins, remain terrible things whatever the reasons. The Native Americans died in thousands fighting to protect their way of life against the European invader. The victor wrote the history and he wrote how difficult it was for them and how much they suffered and basically ignored the fate of the Native

American who was reduced to the status of a captive in their own country living in a designated areas cordoned off from mainstream America.

She Wore a Yellow Ribbon begins with Sgt. Tyree bringing in the paymasters stagecoach that has been attacked by Indians with the dead Major Cheadle inside. He hands one of the officers half of a broken arrow. The officer says:

"it's not Kiowa" to which John Wayne says *"and it's not Comanche or Arapaho either."* Then one of the Top Sergeants nudges Tyree to say something *"Sir, these arrows with white and red and yellow bands is a sign of the Southern Cheyenne"* to which Wayne replies *"I seen Bannocks and Snakes use the same colours."* Sgt. Tyree says *"that's very true sir but look at the clan mark on this arrow it's the sign of the dog. That arrow came from the bow of a Southern Cheyenne Dog Soldier."*

These observations made by Tyree would impress upon a child that there are different types of Indian tribes with different traditions. Tyree thereby shows he is somewhat of an authority on Indian culture and he later shows how his knowledge aids him in tight situations. In a later scene he finds a 7th Calvary hat with a feather in it, acknowledging it is the same 'Indians that killed Custer' he is then attacked and after a suspenseful chase escapes by jumping over a ravine. Many of the details are historically correct; there was a large contingent of ex confederate soldiers in the Calvary troop. The character Tyree is himself an ex Confederate Captain. Therefore by rights he has some military authority when he questions the judgment of his superior Union officers because during the civil war they would have been on an equal footing as officer adversaries (some confederate officers were trained at West Point). When an elderly Trooper Smith dies in battle he is buried with a confederate flag. John Wayne the commanding Officer says the eulogy *"His name was Rome Clay, Brigadier General of the Confederate States Army, known to his comrades here as trooper John Smith United States Calvary. A gallant soldier and a Christian gentleman."* Tyree then stays behind with a large group of ex Confederate soldiers to pay their last respects. In this way John Ford makes us aware of the contribution made by the South in the process of closing the frontier and the difference in the Southern Culture and traditions. The Chief of the Cheyenne dog soldiers is called Red Shirt and his warriors are dressed in colourful red shirts. The original Chief Red Shirt was a Sioux who fought at the Battle of Little Big Horn and surrendered with Crazy Horse along with 277 other warriors including Black Elk in May 1877.[129] Black Elk wrote the book 'Black Elk Speaks' which is one of the earliest authorities on Native American culture that reached a mainstream audience in the beginning of the 1930's. At this time there was a growing awareness of Native American culture and realization that the people that experienced that era in American history were starting to die out. As Native American tradition was oral if these participants recollections were not written down and recorded for prosperity they would be lost forever. Despite the opinions about the accuracy of 'Black Elk Speaks' both from the Native American community and the Academic community, the book continues to be an early testament to events that happened at that time. Black Elk is a primary source he did participate in the Battle of the Little Big Horn and he rode with crazy Horse afterwards. He experienced firsthand some of the major events in American history concerning Native Americans.

We owe an immeasurable debt to researchers like John Neihardt who had the foresight to record these Native American testimonies. Fortunately researchers are continuing to give new interpretations to these transcripts, which then give us more insight into what men like Black Elk were actually trying to express at the time. Rio Grande This film centers on a group of settlers who are taken captive by the Indians and are pursued by the Calvary across the Rio Grande. In one scene an officer of French descent comes across the remains of one of the women who has been killed and possibly tortured. We do not see the body only the recoil of horror from the officer as he murmurs "ce barbaric." This scene seems to justify the hunting down and killing of her assailants. The start of the film is very descriptive and gives an ethnic atmosphere by showing a group of captive Indians drumming and singing at night. There is a lot of 'trooping the colors' and showing military discipline as if to empathize that the US Calvary was a legitimate American military force not a bunch of undisciplined brigands and scum committing barbaric acts against the Native Americans during the closing of the frontier. The actors playing Native Americans are authentic and John Wayne plays Capt. Kirby who speaks Native American to the Navajo Scouts (*Wah Hay*) which can be interpreted as a sign of recognition an respect. Again one of the most interesting characters in this film is Trooper Tyree played by Ben Johnson. He has certain traits that would appeal to young boys. He always knows more than his officers know, but makes a big display about how 'out of place' it would be to put them right. He is a good shot and excellent horse rider self-deprecating and always there to help. He accomplishes many daring feats during the film. He is content riding alone and eats beans cold from a can. He is typical role model for young boys, showing his skills and aptitude he is completely at home in the untamed landscape of the Old West and very competent in all he does. His favorite expression during the film in pressing situations is "Get it done Reb" emphasizing his Southern roots.[130] In his role Tyree epitomizes the American pioneer spirit of optimism that seemed to be ingrained in their outlook on life. He comes from a losing side and is demoted from a Confederate officer to the ranks in his former opponent's army and still performs his tasks to the best of his ability. His performances in Fords films are outstanding and his positive portrayals of Sgt. Tyree help reaffirm our faith in the human nature. Ben Johnson said in an interview later in his life that he "stuck to what I was good at during my career" [131] and that shines through in how natural he appears in his film roles.

The Searchers is a classic movie and is now considered one of the very best Westerns ever made. The American Film Institute named it as the greatest western of all time in 2008. Although on its release in 1956 it did not achieve much acclaim. It gives many different impressions of the Native American way of life in comparison to the European settlers. One noticeable scene is when John Wayne desecrates a grave and shoots the eyes out of a Native American corpse. When the actor Ward Bond who plays a Reverend Captain leading the posse says, *"that won't do anything."* Wayne says *"Not for us but for him it means he can't go to heaven."* This scene would be interpreted by young impressionable boys as a sign that Native Americans have another faith and religion very different from their own. Throughout the film Wayne carries his rifle in a case made of tasseled buckskin obviously a Native American design. This symbolizes that he is willing to use Native American items when they are more functional than the traditional equivalent. It also enhances his visual image of being a part of the frontier, i.e. belonging in an environment that was once the sole domain of the Native American. He often uses the phrase 'That'll be the day' when closing an argument with someone. Buddy Holly was inspired to use the term for the title to one of his songs and there was a popular English group in the sixties who called themselves "The Searchers". There are very violent scenes but we do not see the actual violence shown graphically like in the film Little Big man.

There is one telling scene where Wayne and his companion see a troop of Calvary ride towards an Indian village. When John Wayne reaches the village all the people have been killed. You do not see the Calvary do the killing but it is obvious. In another scene Indians who look half-starved and are fleeing through the snow. Some of these scenes in the film have been interpreted as John Ford trying to atone for his previous portrayal of the Native American in his films. These scenes give us a feeling of compassion for the plight of the Native American where they are now portrayed as the persecuted. The Searchers can be seen as a forerunner to the more revisionist films that came later in the mid-sixties under the banner of Counter Culture Westerns.

23. My Lai

Because of the analogy made between the My Lai massacre of November 1968,[132]and the massacre of Indians in the films Little Big Man and Soldier Blue. The massacre played a critical role in the shifting of public opinion concerning the war in Vietnam. These films and the newsreels and press photographs had a profound effect on an already divided American public. After My Lai the public knew the search and destroy missions in Vietnam in some cases meant attacking villages and killing innocent civilians. This had the dual effect of gaining more support for the anti-war movement and because of the films focus on relatively recent American history (1876) sympathy for the Indian civil rights movements also increased.

In this way the various civil rights movements and counter culture groups interacted. As Slotkin states "In the film Little Big Man they; recreate the Battle of Wichita, when Custer and his men ride in over the white snowfields to massacre the village, mercilessly shooting Crabb's wife and the infant on the cradle board as she flees. As in "Soldier Blue" the visual illusions to My Lai are clear and very horrific."[133]

Any half decent person in any country should find it emotionally distressing to read a newspaper and see images of My Lai showing civilians, women and children begging for their lives and then see the images of their murdered corpses stacked in heaps.

This obscene crime against humanity perpetrated by American troops in the name of freedom and liberty is almost too much to bear. To then see it re-enacted on film in a similar incident of slaughter by the same army under the same flag would make anyone's cup run over. In fact one man watching Little Big Man in Holland became so overwhelmed by the village massacre scene that he climbed over the seats towards the screen, tears streaming down his face, shouting:

"They are still doing it in Vietnam; they are still doing it in Vietnam" [134]

There is no evidence to suggest that it was the director's intention to draw direct parallels with events taking place in South East Asia.[135] Little Big Man was not advertised as an anti-establishment film that had parallels to the Vietnam War or that this film has clear social commentary about prejudice and injustice. The film posters show a more comical image of Dustin Hoffman dressed as an Indian warrior leaving us unprepared for the feast of injustices done to Native

Americans and the extreme racial prejudices shown by the white man towards Native Americans.[136] Obviously some people would have been pretty shocked to see the US military clearly portrayed as ruthless barbarians, lacking any form of humanity. Although 'Little Big Man' was released before My Lai became public knowledge. The atrocities were actually happening in Vietnam at the time the film was made and it is possible people were aware of it through connections with relatives serving there and rumours circulated by returning troops. Whatever the build-up to the event, one thing is for certain when these atrocities were exposed in the Life Magazine it became the turning point.

Now even right wing conservatives started to oppose the war. The increased attention events like My Lai received through films like 'Little Big Man' had an effect all over the world. The event described from Holland shows that the similarities were just too blatant to be ignored. Mylai would come to haunt the American military and Chief of Staffs. Only a helicopter crew commanded by Hugh Thompson behaved with any decency and managed to rescue around 16 civilians. Some of the US military officers conducting the investigation were appalled that most of the accused from Charlie Company did not consider themselves guilty of any crime. [137]

The defendants saw their actions on that fatal day as normal conduct. Only Hugh Thompson showed any signs of behavior befitting an officer when he confronted the troops committing the atrocities and ordered his crew to open fire on them if they tried to shoot any of the civilians he rescued from a bunker. He then stood with the group of around 12 to 16 civilians while they were evacuated in two batches. Thompson and his crew were only officially recognized and decorated for their actions thirty years later in 1998. He could have been used at the time to represent some of the integrity and decency that surely the majority of the American troops had. Instead Thompson was seen as a turncoat by the American military that did all in its powers to cover up this awful atrocity.

24. Little Big Man

People were more aware of the injustices against Indians after the Mai Lai massacre became public knowledge because people who knew their history or Native Americans writing letters to magazines and newspapers drew attention to the parallels between these types of films and the Vietnam War. Arthur Penn the director of Little Big Man makes no mention of Vietnam in a Rolling Stone interview just before the film's release. However there is little doubt that the graphic violence experienced in TV along with news reports from Vietnam had an influence on how violence was portrayed in Hollywood. Both Soldier Blue and Little Big Man came out in 1970. This is very crucial because the Indian activist groups, although they had their origins in the sixties, came into the public eye through media coverage of the actions at Alcatraz and Wounded Knee in 1969 and the early 1970s.

The same applies to many bands that used the country rock 'Wild West' look or military Calvary and Civil war uniforms they formed late sixties or early seventies.[138] This was almost four years after Buffalo Springfield was formed which puts Neil Young and Buffalo Springfield clearly in the vanguard. The film 'Little Big man' is one of the classics of the revisionist genre from 1970. The content and visual imagery are major factors in the promotion of Native American history at that time showing a people with a culture that was indigenous to the United States that had almost been totally erased.

Other important associations between this film and Neil Young's persona at that time is the white man dressed as an Indian for a large part of the film and depicted on movie posters. The visual promotion in the media about this film[139] depicts Dustin Hoffman wearing a choker identical to the one worn by Neil Young. One of the other main characters, General Custer is shown wearing a buckskin tasselled Jacket similar to the one worn by David Crosby on the cover of the Déjà vu album. Dustin Hoffman an actor who is widely identified as a personification of the youth culture of the 60's,[140] plays Jack Crabb a veteran of the Battle of the Little Big Horn who is 121 years old.

By creating this last survivor in the film they have connected a seminal event in American frontier history to the present by an eyewitness account. We anticipate an authentic look into one of the major events in American history.[141] He is in a hospital reciting the story to an academic. This gives the beginning of the film an even more enhanced feeling of authenticity. In the film Jack Crabb also becomes the voice of the Indian. This is one of the problems with the revisionist white hero he does not share the tragic fate of the Indian. We presume when we hear the story of the Indian through a white man's eyes the story will be told in the same way the Lakota's would tell about their heritage and their history. As a child, Hoffman survives an Indian attack where both his parents were killed. He is adopted and raised by Indians from another tribe. The Crabb's voice over monologue slowly adopts the voice of the Indian. He goes back and forth between the two cultures during the film giving us what we interpret as a unique insight into their culture. In the film the white man's Wild West is portrayed as a world full of lying, cheating, and hypocrisy.

The Native Americans are portrayed as a people who care about their culture and the nature. They cherish their families and had integrity and dignity far exceeding the European settlers. Other aspects of this film and ¨Soldier Blue¨ is the allegorizing of these historical events with events in Vietnam. They expose our contemporary ignorance of the culture of the Vietnamese that is mirrored by our historical ignorance of the history and culture of the indigenous people of the American continent the Native Americans.[142] These parallels combined with other elements like the civil rights groups and student groups contributed to the strengthening of mainstream support for the anti-war movement. These kinds of films also contributed vastly to changing the historical image of Native Americans. The audience experiences many beautiful scenes in the film depicting Native American villages and decorated tepees and many fine images of young braves in full regalia. The film has many comical episodes in connection with Jack Crabb's relationship to Wild Bill Hickok along with his relationship to the Native Americans 'Berdache' and 'Heyók☐a'. This film is one of my all-time personal favorites with great acting and a formidable music score by John Hammond. The instructor Arthur Penn is absolutely one of the best from that era. In both production and storyline it is definitely a class above 'Soldier Blue'. The film 'Little Big Man' encapsulates the whole atmosphere of the Native American way of life as seen through the eyes of white people.

25. Historical accuracies in the film "Little Big Man"

Crazy Horse and Sitting Bull were Custer's main adversaries and their names will always appear in films and books associated with Custer.[143] There has probably been more research done about George Armstrong Custer than any other American. The battle of the Little Big Horn was the largest defeat suffered by the American military and their adversaries who fought to preserve the Native American way of life. Sitting Bull and Crazy Horse are household names throughout the English speaking world.

As a revisionist film about our collective consciousness concerning the history of the Native American, Little Big Man has a prominent position. The film was released at the height of the Vietnam War and the parallels between the behaviour of the soldiers in this film and the American soldiers responsible for the Mai Lai massacre is deeply disturbing even though the details emerged after the film was released. These parallels became very apparent to audiences round the world and increased international support for the anti-war movement.

The portrayal of Custer and the re-enacting of Custer's massacre of a defenseless Cheyenne village in the Battle of Washita (1868)[144] and his demise at the Battle of Little Big Horn (1876)[145] appears to be historically correct on many points. One exception is the character of Jack Crabb portrayed by Dustin Hoffmann who narrates the story. The film includes many historical figures like Wild Bill Hickok who Neil Young wrote a song about Ode the Wild Bill, George Armstrong Custer once said "I could be an Indian."[146] Showing that even during that period it was desirable to some European Americans to adopt the Indian identity. The portrayal of Custer as a despot who split up his force against advice and teased his Crow army scouts calling them women because they wanted to sing their death chant before going into battle is accurate according to some sources. I find the language an euphemisms used by Native Americans at that time very poignant, to me it is sometimes has a Shakespearean richness, much of Macbeth is about visions and dreams as in 'Black Elk Speaks'. A good example (in the historical account of the event not in the film) when a Crow Scout ¨Half Yellow Face¨ tried to warn Custer about the size of the enemy camp with the lines:

"You and I are both are going home today by a road that we do not know."[147]

It is possible Neil Young is familiar with some Native American vernacular from the works of Gary Snyder's who uses the Native American terminology,[148] or by talking to Native American's. Neil has had the Native American bass player Rick Rosas in his bands on several occasions. They worked together on the Chrome Dreams Continental Tour – Europe 2008 that consisted of 21 shows in nine countries. It is quite probable that they had some long conversations. Rick says that:

"Neil does not discuss that kind of thing but seems to like Native American things. So maybe he was a Native American in a previous life." Rick also mentioned the cigar store Indian *"Neil always like to have him on stage and when it disappeared once he went to great lengths to retrieve it"*

Neil Young acknowledged Rick's Native American heritage when he introduced him on stage in Berlin in 2009. I later learned from Rusties that there is a Native American dimension to his life that he does not advertise much at least not in Europe. This can be seen in his use of Native American dancers at his Bridge School benefit concerts and the fact that he is a blood brother to a Native American. There is a real feeling of authenticity in this film not least because of the ambience created by John Hammond's soundtrack. The rustic acoustic guitar sounds twanging and grinding emphasizes a rough and ready atmosphere of an unsophisticated, hard way of life. That sound coupled with the scenes of the frontier towns emulates the Old West in a very convincing way. This music represents the period more accurately than the orchestrated theme music of previous Westerns. Hammond uses contemporary instruments similar to the ones made in that period. Photographs of these can be found with cowboys playing them. [149]The acoustic guitar Neil Young prefers to use is the Country and Western model made by the Martin Guitar Company established in 1833.[150]

The character known as Little Big Man did exist at that time but as a Native American, not as a European captive. He was a cousin to Crazy Horse. He was involved in the armed conflict that was fought against the white man and when he surrendered in 1877 he became an Indian scout. Little Big man was directly involved in the incident where Crazy Horse was killed and some accounts name him as the perpetrator of the deed but fearing retribution it was attributed to a Calvary trooper.

In 1976 'Life' magazine devoted a special section called "To our Indian Heritage" with a revisionist accounts of the Indian wars which emphasized white responsibility and acknowledged Indian leaders like Crazy Horse as "Great Men" not savages.[151] One cannot overemphasize the importance of an historical figure like Crazy Horse in Native American culture and history. He can be compared with Mohammed Ali in African American culture. They both fought against great adversity and won. They both showed a complete lack of compromise and stayed loyal to their beliefs. There is a huge monument to Crazy Horse under construction close to Mount Rushmore the location symbolizing his rightful place among great American leaders.

Crazy Horse is the name of the band most associated with Neil Young throughout his career. Use of this name is a major element in the associations that people make to Native Americans even if they make the associations subconsciously. It familiarizes people with the Native American names and traditions. In many cases the names are connected to historical events that then come up in a discussion. Even if it is only "Hey man who is Crazy Horse?" To which the reply can either be: "That's Neil Young's band" or "He was the guy who beat Custer"

26. Soldier Blue

Both these films had the extra dimensions in their music: the soundtrack to "Little Big Man" by John Hammond was a rustic acoustic authentic western sound, while the lyrics to the title song "Soldier Blue" were written and emotionally sung by the Native American Buffy Saint Marie (she is originally from Canada where Indians are called 'People of the First Nation') [152]

"I wrote this song as the title theme for the movie Soldier Blue and it became a hit in Europe, Japan and Canada during the summer of 1971. Chris Birkett plays guitar but the movie disappeared from U.S. theatres real fast, so few Americans are familiar with it. As there's a difference between love and rape, the same differences exist in how one views their country. "Soldier Blue" is not about loving one's "nation state"; it's about loving the natural environment in which all nations are related as children of the Sacred ."

"I can stand upon a hill at dawn, look all around me, Feel her surround me, Soldier Blue, Can't you see her life has just begun, It's beating inside us, Telling us she's here to guide us".

The verse appeals to the soldier to try to change:

"Soldier Blue, Soldier Blue Can't you see that there's another way to love her." [153]

Here Buffy Saint Marie says love of country is not about love of the Nation State but of the natural environment. This reinforces early statement about how Native Americans are perceived to be connected to nature. Verse four illustrates the sentiment of the song and fits into the Hippie ideology of the sixties period that related to and in many cases adopted the Native Americans relationship to nature. Buffy Saint

Marie's career merges with Neil Young's on several occasions. She played the clubs in Canada in 1964 alongside other emerging Canadian artists: Joni Mitchell, Leonard Cohen and Neil Young. She wrote the protest song Universal Soldier during this period. One can clearly see the difference in style between Universal Soldier and Soldier Blue. She and Jack Nitzsche got married in 1980. Jack Nitzsche worked on Neil Young's early albums and played on Harvest. Here we see how certain elements in Neil Young's career converged and intertwined. Buffy Saint Marie and the group Redbone were the only Native American artists who achieved wide recognition during the sixties. The point she makes about the film not being in theatres long in the US has parallels with Redbones hit released We were all Wounded at Wounded Knee about the massacre of Sioux Indians at Wounded Knee in 1890. The single reached number one in the UK and Europe but was withheld in the US and then banned on several radio stations.

27. Civil Rights Groups

American society was divided by the events taking place during the sixties. In the early sixties with Kennedy there was optimism. Middle America was harvesting the effects of post-war economic prosperity. The Rock and Roll that started in the fifties became popular again in the sixties and evolved into 'Beatlemania' in 1964. "By mid-decade, it was evident to all Americans that something powerful was shaking the fundamental structures of American life. This only intensified as the decade progressed." [154]

The counter culture was illuminating the world by transcending borders with their music, philosophy and lifestyle. They demanded more freedom and change. To make their protest, they combined the creative element of music that reached the mainstream with mass demonstrations in the streets. The major factors that contributed to this were the civil rights groups: The largest group was the Black Power civil rights group under the leadership of Dr. Martin Luther King. This group consisted of African American descendants of slaves demanding their long overdue equal rights. Like the Native Americans they have a long history of racial discrimination and segregation. Radical groups like the Black Panthers influenced young Native Americans to form AIM.[155] The forming of groups and organizations is a critical point in a democracy. It shows you have the right to be heard. If you can get the majority behind you or a considerable amount of the majority you can contribute to changing things. The organization then becomes the mouthpiece that speaks for the group. The power of the individual during the sixties was optimized by joining together in groups and political organizations these groups slowly started to acquire the legal, political and economic clout to take on the system. It was the actions and interactions between these groups that helped to influence government policy and changed public opinion. The Black Civil Rights Movement was the major force in the fight for civil rights in America in the sixties. Through actions like the Memphis Sanitation Workers strike, they slowly managed to change the attitude of whites towards African Americans. Their actions were an inspiration for others to follow. Under the leadership of Martin Luther King they proved non-violent protest could achieve results. To achieve their goals many paid the highest price. Shortly after the Sanitation strike, Martin Luther King was assassinated in Memphis. A disproportionate number African Americans served in Vietnam. The Vietnam memorial in Washington shows that their participation and casualties were discordantly high compared to the white counterparts. One of the African Americans who served in 1966 was Clarence Fitch:

"The militancy really grew after Martin Luther King got killed in '68. It made black people really angry. You remember the riots after Dr. Kings death was some of the fiercest, and the brothers took that up in Vietnam. People changed after that. People were saying it doesn't pay to be non-violent and benevolent. There were a lot of staff NCOs, the type of so called Negro that would be telling you to be patient, just do your job, pull yourself up by the bootstraps. So we called them Uncle Toms and that was that. People were saying, "I'm black and I'm proud. I'm not going to be an Uncle Tom"

Fitch talks later about the solidarity there was among the soldiers in

Vietnam and he confirms more of my points about the casualty rate. I will use another quote as he is representative of two major groups in the sixties, the African American minority that were fighting for civil rights and he is one of the soldiers fighting in Vietnam, he continues:

"There was the whole Black Power thing. There was Black Power salutes and handshakes and Afros and beads. It was a whole atmosphere. All that was a way of showing our camaraderie, like brothers really hanging together. When a new brother came into the unit, we used to really reach out for the guy, show him the ropes and tell him what's happening. It was like togetherness that I ain't seen since. I think people really listened to Martin Luther King. We didn't hear his speech about Vietnam until much later, but somehow or another I got a copy of the speech, and we was really impressed. He talked about how blacks were dying in Vietnam at a greater rate, and he was the first person we really ever heard say that, even though it was something we knew." [156]

Here Fitch makes a number of points that are relevant, 'Black Power' and the atmosphere it created combined with the sense of togetherness that seems to run through the sixties. 'He has never seen it since.' A lot of people I have quoted refer to this element of togetherness that was found in the sixties, 'where people cared about each other.' Obviously Fitch is in a war zone and different rules apply. There is usually a sense of 'brotherhood' among soldiers in any war zone as survival depends on teamwork. His comments about Martin Luther King are enlightening as he appears to be the first public person to mention the fact that blacks were dying at a greater rate in the Vietnam conflict. Black Civil rights, marches in the US combined with student and civil unrest against the Vietnam War became a focal point during the 1960s. This growing antiwar movement was supported by the counter culture. As Marwick stated: *"Vietnam became the great universal issue, binding together protests within America over race, poverty, consumerism, and alleged repression of student freedoms, and providing a focal point for youth and anti-establishment protests throughout Europe"* [157]

In America, the government fiercely opposed these protests with Riot

Police and National Guardsmen. As the war in Vietnam escalated, the antiwar demonstrations became more frequent. The confrontations were sometimes exceedingly violent. This anti-American worldwide publicity was the antithesis of what the America government were trying to portray: ¨The land of the free,¨ leading the world in the new technological age: ¨The Space Age¨, a new frontier. With the Apollo Space program America hoped to beat the Russians in the race to the moon. At every launch there was the image of the American flag on the side of a big white Saturn V Rocket and the letters U.S.A. going up your TV screen as it lifted off. This was followed by news broadcasts of events in Vietnam, newsreel images of American soldiers burning villages and driving off weeping villagers clutching their babies and meager possessions or viewer saw fire fights where American soldiers were wounded and dying. [158]Combined with domestic reports of National guardsmen in gas masks charging demonstrators. All these events triggered a reaction that made Vietnam one of the key issues that haunted the American collective consciousness throughout the 20th century.

28. The Native Americans

The parallels between the treatment of Vietnamese civilians by American troops in the sixties and the treatment of Native Americans in the previous century were very clear. This caused a revision in their role in American history and encouraged the public to support Indians in the fight for civil rights. Film directors used the comparison to Vietnam in films like Little Big Man and Soldier Blue which few criticized for false sentiment' this greatly strengthened the Native American cause.[159] One of the major factors in influencing the revision of the role of the Native American in American history was the genre of the 'Counter Culture Western'. The Indians were now portrayed as the victims of injustice as opposed to their previous role as the savage aggressor. Another major factor in these turbulent times came from the media: the nightly news reports from Vietnam shown on television dwarfed the Hollywood dramas where violence and realism were concerned. Horrific scenes like

135

the one of the South Vietnamese Police chief shooting a Vietcong suspect's brains out on camera. The victim falls with a jet of blood squirting from the wound. Another news report shows a naked little girl running towards the camera covered in napalm. The effect of these gruesome images broadcast around the world was that it brought the reality of the war into people's living rooms. These images spread anti American sentiment and contributed to growing anti-war movements worldwide. [160]

29. Film Censorship

Film censorship had to change radically during the sixties because of what was happening in the society. The rules and restrictions not only on the sex and violence but also the political content about themes like inter racial relations. The world became transformed things that were legal in the UK were still illegal in the USA and vice versa. At the opening of the decade in the UK there was a new wave of books, plays and films like 'Saturday Night and Sunday Morning' that focused on the daily life of the working classes in Britain. It was the film "A Taste of Honey" that transcended barriers and boundaries concerning race and sexual orientation and later the film "Cathy Come Home" highlighted the lack of housing for young working class couples.

Later when there were the drug busts of celebrities like the Rolling Stones, who were found guilty of possessing amphetamine that they legally bought in a chemist in Italy while on tour. This resulted in the famous editorial in The Times: Do we break the Butterfly on the wheel? The establishment came under attack and almost everything that had previously been taboo was now open to public debate.

In the USA the media and entertainment industry also played a major part in this debate. Driven mainly by the profit motive it would put out whatever would sell. The emergence of Rock Bands like Buffalo Springfield in the mid-sixties around LA, contributed significantly to the atmosphere. Worried about the increasing teen and hippie presence along the Sunset Strip the municipal authorities put out a curfew aimed at young crowds. The teens demonstrated and the police waded in with batons causing a riot. The Buffalo Springfield released the protest song about the event called "For what it's Worth." with the lyrics:

"There's a man with a gun over there, telling me I got to beware."

These words expressed the feeling of fear that had come to the streets. The main point here is that many changes are taking place especially in the media and how the general public viewed the war and demonstrations. The establishment is no longer able to quietly club demonstrators and lock up rock starts without getting media attention and in some case public outcry. During this period people were exposed to events that are more violent and extreme in the daily news reels.

 The freedom of the press in Vietnam resulted in people getting a very clear view of what was going on over there. Margaret Thatcher would limit the access of the press to the Falklands War because of the lesson learned in Vietnam. Public opinion could put pressure on political decision making that in turn could affect military strategy. It is very hard to increase military action when domestically you have massive public protest. The Kent State demonstration s at Ohio was in answer to Nixon's intensifying the war by bombing Cambodia. Censorship especially in films had to be changed because the reality of the war was depicted far more graphically in newsreels than violence was in the movies.

30. American Indian Movement (AIM)

In the preface to the reprint of the 1969 book, Custer Died for your Sins Native American author Vine Deloria, Jr. states: *"The early seventies saw the spread of the American Indian Movement as a tidal wave of protest. AIM now seems to be in a dormant if not comatose stage, but its accomplishments cannot be underestimated. AIM created a feeling of solidarity among Indians which has now increased and entrenched itself during the intervening years. Most important for the long run have been good educational organizations that have taken root among Indians in*

recent years." [161] A copy of a New York Times Magazine article by
Deloria from 1970 is reproduced in Red Power commending AIM's
occupation of Alcatraz. This statement shows the size of the Indian
population and the images of Native Americans people have from TV.

" *The Alcatraz news stories are somewhat shocking to non-Indians. It is
difficult for most Americans to comprehend that there still exists a living
community of nearly one million Indians in this country. For many
people, Indians have become a species of movie actor periodically
dispatched to the happy hunting grounds by John Wayne on the 'Late,
Late Show' There are some 315 Indian tribal groups in 26 states still
functioning as quasi – sovereign nations under treaty status.*"

Here he tries to make people aware that there is a large Indian
population, living in 315 different tribal groups. Many people only
associate them with people hunted by John Wayne in films on TV. The
Native American Indian rights group AIM was founded in 1968,[162] by a
group consisting of among others Dennis Banks and Clyde Bellecourt.
The newly formed group that had been inspired by the Black Panthers
took as their manifesto books like Red Power,[163] and Custer Died for
Your Sins.[164] Red Power defined the background for the 'American
Indian Revolution' thus: "*For almost 500 years Indians have been
fighting defensively for their right to exist for their freedom, their lands,
their means of livelihood, their organizations and societies, their beliefs,
their ways of life, their personal security, their very lives. Those who still
remain after so many generations of physical and cultural genocide
continue to be oppressed by shattering problems, most of them created
by the intruder, conqueror, and dispossessor, the white man. In the
United States of the 1970's Indian Americans are the poorest of the
poor.*" [165]

They go on to point out that Native American life expectancy is more
than six years under the national average and that their annual income
is $1,500 which is 75% less that the national average and $1000 below
that of an average African American family. Their unemployment rate at
that time was ten times more that the national average. There were a

lot of things to fight for at that time as I have pointed out in other examples.[166] AIM was an inspiration to young Native Americans all over the United States. AIM lobbied for their cause and especially tried to take the power from the white administrators of the Indian Bureau of Affaires claiming that Indians were being governed like 'colonial subjects' [167]

"Ever since the White man reached the new world he has recognized 'Indian problems', though usually not recognizing he created them himself".

This was one of the main issues in the Indian civil rights movement. That Indians had handled their own affairs for hundreds of years before the white man came. Gary Snyder pointed out that America had existed for thousands of years before the white man came without problems and the way we treat the environment has had a devastating effect within only eighty years. Snyder has promoted adopting Native American approaches when dealing with nature. In their call for justice AIM accuses the Federal Government of treaty violations with their policies of 'termination' towards the Indians that resulted in land confiscation and loss of hunting and fishing rights. They claimed the Indian land in California was taken from them illegally in 1853 and in a way that was against the principles of the constitution. Here you can see the young Native American academics have learned how modern Americans see their history and are formulating their claims in such a manner that they cannot be ignored. In addition to the legal claims, they come with their own cultural and moral argument that:

"No amount of money can buy mother earth; therefore, the California Land Claims Case has no meaning. The Earth is our Mother and we cannot sell her." [168]

One of AIM´s highest priorities was police brutality, *"it was primarily a grassroots effort to stop police brutality against Indian people, to stop friends and relatives from being beaten."* [169]
The group formed a militant leadership similar to the Black Panthers

only theirs was founded on a respect for tribal traditions. They said they were willing to die for their people. [170]AIM started to use confiscated land that was still theirs by rights as venues for staging demonstrations. The island of Alcatraz was known internationally as the prison that housed America's most notorious gangsters like Al Capone. The penitentiary was closed down in 1963 and in the autumn of 1969 AIM occupied it as the first major action for their cause. Indian College activists and families including small children held Alcatraz for 18 months. Native American author Vine Deloria Jr. stated: "*Alcatraz was a big enough symbol that for the first time this century Indians were taken seriously,*"

Alcatraz was a universal symbol of incarceration. The occupation by AIM showed the Indians new determination to go on the offensive and throw off their shackles to achieve their rights. There were cultural obstacles for the Native Americans to present their case. They have an oral tradition, their languages are very different, and although some sound similar, the words have a completely different meaning. In the sixties, young college educated Native Americans not only understood the language of the autocrats that had been ruling over them and suppressing their culture but more importantly they started to appreciate the legal aspects of certain issues and started to demand their rights through a system that had to recognize their legitimate claims. AIM started to fight for Native American civil rights and treaty rights.

"Indian scholars and intellectuals, they are riding on the winds of change that are abroad in today's world, demanding and receiving the attention of non-Indians".

The book accepts that it was the struggle of the African American that helped developments during the sixties or at least increased white awareness: "Attracted first to the struggle of the blacks, Americans have become seriously attentive to the status and needs of all minorities within the nation" [171]

In 1973, AIM occupied Wounded Knee on the Pine Ridge Lakota Sioux reservation. This was the historical site of the Wounded Knee massacre on the 29th December 1890. This massacre was still within recent history, only 80 years had passed, it was by no means 'ancient history'. The Wounded Knee occupation by AIM resulted in vast media coverage that usually included the historical facts accompanied by pictures of frozen bodies from the massacre like that of the Native American Chief Big Foot. Deloria gives a poignant account of visiting the historical site as a child: *"The most memorable event of my early childhood."* Visiting the site of this massacre is one of the most memorable events he carries with him through life. This shows the status that this 'shrine 'has for native Americans. The place where the 7th Calvary, Custer's regiment took their vengeance. I would propose that this was why AIM occupied "Wounded Knee" they knew what the act would symbolize for Native Americans. *"The most memorable event of my early childhood was visiting Wounded Knee where 200 Sioux, including women and children, were slaughtered in 1890 by troopers of the Seventh Calvary in what is believed to have been a delayed act of vengeance for Custer defeat."* [172]

He goes on to say that the wounded were left for three days in a blizzard after which those who were still alive were saved. The massacre was still vividly etched in the minds of many of the older reservation people, but it was difficult to find anyone who wanted to talk about it. This shows some of the historical injustices done to the Native Americans. Almost every event where villages or settlements were attacked and the warriors were absent, the defenseless occupants were slaughtered and it became known as a battle. Every time the Calvary had losses in engagements with Native Americans it became known as a massacre by savages. It is important to have an understanding of this in relation to the actions and demands made by AIM. Through historical images of Chief Big Foot, released by the press in relation with AIM's occupation of the Pine Ridge Agency at Wounded Knee the public became more conscious of their history and the injustices that had been done and covered over for more than 50 years.

31. Indian Civil Rights and the Counter Culture

I have described a visit to Wounded Knee by Johnny Cash, where one could see on the film he was clearly moved.[173] Native Americans were also becoming more visible on the music scene:

"Among the young city and university Indians particularly, loyalty to their individual tribes and to the Indian people in general began to blaze high during the sixties....Indian protest songs, sung by Johnny Cash, a descendent of Cherokee,[174] Floyd Westerman, a Sioux and Buffy Sainte-Marie, a Cree inspired them…..Indian students pressured for the introduction of Indian studies." [175]

The Native American band Redbone released the song *"We were all Wounded at Wounded Knee"* this was banned in the US but reached number one in the UK.[176] This showed not only was it a great song but there was a sincere sense of solidarity in the world for the Native American cause. Redbone had written a song about an event that concerned the Native Americans and it was not even allowed airplay in their own country. Whereas English people that had very little cultural connection to the event could hear it on the radio. As it was in the number one spot it reached a very large audience In the UK and in this way people there also learned something about Native American culture. This is a very important factor as it contributes to keeping the culture alive as Deloria states:

"The takeover of Alcatraz is to many Indian people a demonstration of pride in being an Indian and a dignified, yet humorous protest against current conditions existing on the reservations and in the cities. It is this special pride and dignity, the determination to judge life according to one's own values, and the unconquerable conviction that the tribes will not die that has always characterized Indian people as I have known them"

Here he shows that people could start taking pride in being an Indian and although Neil Young was not an Indian the Comanche War Jackets he wore in the Buffalo Springfield days reflected a warrior culture. That must have been encouraging for Indian kids watching TV that not everyone was dressed as a cowboy in the rock music business. The other part of my contention is that Neil Young contributed to the cause in general by using Native American regalia and bringing the visual image of the Native American into the public imagination through Record Covers, TV and magazines. When writing about counterculture or civil rights groups the sixties you cannot avoid Rock Music. Because these bands contributed to what was happening at the time which makes them interrelated. According to author Donald L. Fixco whose writings contributed to the rewriting of Native American history in the twentieth century recalls how he felt as a 17 year old in the sixties when AIM was formed: "The rise in AIM was important to those of us who were coming of age during the late 1960's and 1970's. Native American intellectuals like Deloria from the late sixties and early seventies helped start an 'Indian Renaissance' that led to the creation of Native study programs during the rest of the twentieth century." [177]

One study done in the nineties showed there were 100 American Indian studies, programs, departments and canters in the US and Canada. When he began to study 20th century Indian history in the late 70s very few scholars knew much about it. In his closing statement he says: "On the one hand, the 20th century was not entirely good for Indians. There were decades when being an Indian or looking dark skinned was a curse and light skinned Indians denied being native at all. On the other hand, the late 1960's and the 1970's were proud times – with the advent of hippies, New Agers, and the early environmental movement, it seemed as though even white people wanted to be Indian." [178]

This is a vital source as he clearly states that because of the advent of the various counter cultures. This was a proud time for Indians. This is one of my main points because these groups and artists like Neil Young adopted Native American imagery. Native Americans became more accepted and experienced a sincere interest in their culture and way of life. However this interest sometimes had another side as Deloria experienced when he was executive director of the National Congress of Indians. During his three year term, whites who had discovered Indian descent appeared at his office almost daily. Cherokee was the most popular tribe. At first he was defensive about being a Sioux and that these white people had a pedigree that was so much more 'respectable' than his. However, eventually he came to understand their need to identify as partially Indian. It was based mainly on mythical beliefs about Indians. All but one of these people claimed it on the grandmother's side, which meant if you did a projection backwards, you find that all tribes were female for the first 300 years of the white occupation! Deloria speculates on the reason these whites wanted to be part Indian: *"Is it because they are afraid to be classified foreigners. Do they need some blood tie with the frontier and its dangers in order to experience what it means to be American? Or is it an attempt to avoid facing the guilt they bear for the treatment of the Indian?"* [179]

Part of the reason might have been that Native American was seen as people that had a connection with the nature in the middle of an increasingly artificial consumer society. There was a negative dimension that some people wanted to be Native American or like Johnny Cash claimed they were part Native American because of preconceived ideas about the culture and spiritual beliefs and their way of life. What Deloria calls "mainly mythical beliefs about Indians?" But in general groups interacted and although they sometimes they did not agree with each other like when Hippies showed up at "fish ins" where Native Americans were trying to fish in areas off their reservations but included in their treaty rights. The fishermen did not agree with the Hippie philosophy but the participation of young white middle class kids could result in less police brutality, therefore they became tolerated supporters. At concerts and festivals any Native American ancestry was displayed proudly as seen in the audience at Monterey Pop festival. Here Mickey Dolenz of "The Monkees" a band that generated huge media coverage, displayed his Native American ancestry by wearing a full Indian War Bonnet in the style of the plains Indians. Jimi Hendrix symbolically wore an Indian headband at Monterey while performing to show his Cherokee heritage. The Hippie music festivals had much in common with Indian Pow Wows. The people gathered in huge crowds for some days, they were transitory living in tents or sleeping under the stars. They heard music, chanted together sharing their food, and passing round the "peace pipe". They wanted to get away from the artificial synthetic environment that was starting to dominate the urban culture, making them feel they were surrounded by plastic.[180] This feeling of being engulfed in plastic encouraged some members of the counter culture to look for places to live that were unspoiled. The musicians moved to Laurel Canyon. Some of the beats hung out at the Big Sur. These natural idylls slowly eroded as the locations became more popular with the mainstream. To promote this back to nature ideal events like the 'Gathering of the Tribes' adopted many of the Native American images and rituals like Pow Wows in their advertising and execution of the event. One of their goals was to liberate people and help them free themselves from the repressive constraints of the conservative system and try and return to some of the collective social experiences that were previously prominent in Western societies. For example the gatherings that could be found in Europe during the middle ages at fairs and markets. In America it was the Pow Wow or gathering of the Tribes like the one 100 years earlier where various Native American tribes had converged at an agreed place to try and forget their differences and unite against the common foe. They celebrated with feasting and dancing.

It was during this gathering that Custer initiated the Battle of the Little Big Horn under the misapprehension that he would be facing a small group he left behind his Hoshkiss Gattling guns and split up his force. His participation enabled the victorious warriors to incorporate the events from the battle into their celebration. Custer is without doubt one of the most researched American historical figures from that period. Neil Young named his band after the Native American Chief Crazy Horse who helped to defeat Custer at the battle of the Little Big Horn. This Battle was a major victory for the Native Americans and is still the largest defeat the American army had ever suffered. In the same spirit of paying homage to battles Stephen Still's named his first band 'Manassas' after the first battle of the American civil war 1861 a second battle was fought in 1862 both times the Confederates won over the Union troops.[181] There is a tendency in retrospect to turn the sixties into a romantic era: The way Neil Young describes the period in some of his songs. However many of them were written at the time therefore are reflective of the zeitgeist back then.

In another context songs like *"Marrakesh Express"* opened up countries like Morocco and Algeria that had long been patronized by the Beats and other authors during the 1950´s and early 1960´s, now there was a large influx of long haired young people crammed into VW busses.

Top bands of that era played at benefits and supported other civil rights causes making their fans aware of the political circumstances. At Monterey Pop Festival David Crosby of the Byrd's spoke out about the Kennedy assassination conspiracy. There was a very vibrant active interaction between the bands themselves and their supporters not only through records but also through the live performance and noticeably the causes they supported. This can be seen by the last benefit in support of Native Americans the Buffalo Springfield were booked to appear at. Many of the groups like the Airplane and artists that Neil Young personally knew like Buffy St. Marie were present.[182] Young Native Americans are now clearly interacting with the counterculture and starting to use some of the methods utilized in the sixties to provoke change. They have occupied Alcatraz and turned it into a symbol of American unity. Note how the university students are pressuring for Native American studies to be introduced. At the same time some of the biggest bands around at the time are supporting them with benefit concerts. For a short period the plight of the Native Americans and their place in society and the history books became a cause that was close to people's hearts. The revision of the role of the Native American that took place in the sixties facilitated a world of change that is described in the statements of two academics; Della Warrior and Shelly L. Smith. The following statements and extracts are taken from the book 'Beyond Red Power' this was published in 2007 to look back on the period since 'Red Power' which was published in 1970. The first extract is from Sherry L. Smith who is associated with Native American rights, Sherry confirms my theory that non-Indians in the counter culture did contribute towards making a difference. Neil Young falls into this category through his use of Native American Imagery and the use of Native American names, for records, bands and places where he lived. Regardless of how small or effective his contribution was it helped facilitate the change that Della Warrior describes in her final statement. Furthermore, Sherry L. Smith goes on to say that it became harder to distinguish the aims and interests of the different groups as the boundaries between them became porous. This has also been one of my contentions that by using Native American imagery as Neil Young did, you expose it to your audience who come specially to see you plus a larger audience that you reach through the use of the mass media. Sherry goes on to say that historians that try to separate them from one another do a disservice to the intersections that took place. She points out the 'binding' that held these groups together was the shared values, viewpoints and politics. What I see as part of the core of my research is this interaction between people and groups that have common values. They sometimes unintentionally converged on 'intersections' and in that way become united. This is the reason I have used these elements in my research because they are all interrelated. They did have an influence on each other in the sixties. For Neil Young it was musical success and the possibility to contribute politically because of events that were happening to young people. Stills and Young were very young at the time of Buffalo Springfield so they identified strongly with their peer group. They have always done this, through their music. A lot of people heard that music at that time and a lot of people saw their shows, like when they supported the Stones at Shea Stadium. What Sherry says here fits very well into this perspective: "Native activist gained allies who often demonstrated little genuine understanding of / or deep commitment to treaty rights. Their presence though, helped to bring Indians' issues to larger audiences and to broaden support for significant policy change."

"Non-Indians supported Indian rights movements with their money, pens, talents and skills and, in demonstrations with their bodies. This interest and these actions mattered." "By the late 1960s the boundaries among these identifiable groups and interests were porous. Influences spread in all directions. What activists shared was a deep discontent with conventional values, viewpoints, and politics. The tendency of historians and others, in retrospect, to separate them from one another does a disservice to the sometimes tenuous and temporary, but powerful intersections that took place."

I will close with some comments by Della Warrior, the essence of what she says I have read countless times in various books about Native Americans growing up in the sixties. Native Americans that were denied their own culture now have their own education system and have taken control of the running of their lives. She has been engaged in issues evolving around Indian education since the 1960s. She can look back over 40 years with a great sense of pride and achievement: "When I attended college in the early 1960s, there were probably fewer than a thousand Indian students enrolled across the entire United States (today only 17% of American Indian students who graduate from high school go on to college). There were twelve of us in my high school graduating class. Eight of us were Native Americans, and of that eight, two went on to earn college degrees."

"I was the first person in my extended family to get a high school education. Out of all my aunts and uncles children, my mother's generation, I was the first one to graduate from High School and then go to college."

She goes on to illustrate how things have changed since then in day-to-day things like services by making a comparison to when she was a child and how her mother inspired her. Della starts with an example from the present day situation followed by how she remembered things as a child. I put in the whole statement here because it gives a good illustration of how things were for her growing up as a Native American child: *"Today if you go to visit a tribal headquarters, you will see Indian people running their own governments and in control of nearly all the services, these provide. But it was not always that way. The young people who are coming up today take it for granted. They think it has always been that way, but that is not the case."*

"You are twelve, and you walk down the hallway of the Pawnee Indian Agency office and look around. You see that the only Indians working there are a couple of secretaries and the janitor. Then you go with your aunt over to the Indian hospital because you need to get some immunizations and she needs some meds. Again, you notice that the only Indians working there are in menial positions. When you get back to Red Rock, you begin looking around at the little businesses there – the grocery store, three small cafes, a couple of service stations, a hardware store, a post office, and then a co-op where the farmers bring their wheat crops. And you notice that there are no Indians running any of these businesses, even though the town is predominately Indian, because that was how it was started. It was originally set up as a reservation. So you begin to wonder about this. Why is this? Why, in a community that is predominantly Native, don't we have any doctors or nurses or teachers or principals? Why aren't we running the café? Why don't some of us own the grocery store? You begin thinking about this, so you ask your mother…..Your mother tells you "Well that's the way it is now. That is why you need to go to school. and maybe you can do something to help your people – go to school and come back here and help in some way."

Della Warrior was married to Clyde Warrior one of the founding members of the NIYC and she mentions how he would visit college campuses in 1961 stirring things up saying such purportedly outrageous things like: *"Let us make our own mistakes. We couldn't possibly do any worse that the federal government." "We have a right to make our own choices and decisions. We don't need the Bureau of Indian Affairs doing this for us" "We could be "educated" without losing our indianness." "Our heritage and culture are important. They need to be incorporated into the school curriculum" "Indians need to be able to determine their own destiny. They need to run their own educational systems. They need to take charge of their future"*

To this Della summarizes;

"Today Clyde's statements sound very logical; they make total sense. But at the time, they were considered radical." "All Clyde ever wanted - this man whom so many people called a radical and found so threatening – was to ensure that Indians could improve their standard of living without having to abandon their 'Indianness' "

This extract from Della Warrior shows how it was growing up as A Native American in the USA during the sixties. She states at the beginning how different the present day situation is to the one she describes from her childhood. This testimony combined with that of Sherry L. Smith support my thesis that non-Indians like Neil Young in the counter culture helped make a difference. I am very grateful for the material and encouraging comments I received from the Rusties, they helped show how things were back then and the connection between Neil Young and the Native Americans today.

I hope we can be in agreement that Neil Young did in some way contribute to the Native American civil rights cause in the sixties through the use of Native American imagery in his work. I realize that some questions are left unanswered but I hope some of the examples I have made in the book have helped the reader reach some of their own conclusions about the period.

Meanwhile the genre of the Western movie continues to grow and develop. They seem to go in and out of style and when you believe they have finally been laid to rest, a new one comes along. The Western is truly an intricate part of the short and violent history of America. This history is constantly undergoing reassessment as time goes by. During the sixties a lot of things changed in our perception of what history and life were all about.

Bibliography

Bloom, A. (2001). Long Time Gone. London: Weidenfeld & Nicolson.

Brown, D. (2007). Bury My Heart at Wounded Knee. London: Folio.

Castro, M. (1983). Interpreting the Indian. Norman: university of Oklahoma.

Cheewa James (1995) Catch the Whisper of the Wind. Health Communications, Florida.

Conlan, R. (1995). Tribes of the Northern Plains. New York: Time Life.

Corral, M. o. (1966). Great Western Indian Fights. Lincoln: university of Nebraska.

Cronyn, G. W. (1991). American Indian Poetry. New York: Fawcett.

Cutler, C. L. (2002). Tracks that Speak. Boston: Houghton Mifflin.

Davis, R. (1995). Strong Hearts. Turin: Aperture.

Debo, A. (2003). History of the Indians of the United States. London: Folio.

Downing, D. (1994). Neil Young. A Dreamer of Pictures. London: Bloomsbury.

Echard, W. (2005). Poetics of Energy. Indiana: Indiana University.

Elliott, M. A. (2007). Custerology. Chicago: University of Chicago.

Faragher, R. V. (2007). Frontiers , A Short History of the American West. New York: Yale University.

Fowler, C. &. (2007). Beyond Red Power. US: School for Advanced

Research.

Furay, R. (1998). For What it's Worth. London: Rogan House.

Gallop, A. (2001). Buffalo Bill's Wild West. UK: Sutton Publisher.

Grant, S. (1998). Essential Neil Young. London: Chameleon.

Green, R. (1999). Encyclopedia of Native North America. British Museum: British Museum Press.

Grey, H. C. (2005). Buffalo Bill last of the Great Scouts . Lincoln: University of Nebraska.

Havighurst, W. (1957). Buffalo Bill's Great Wild west Show. New York: Random House.

Heatley, M. (1997). Neil Young in his own Words. UK: Page Brothers.

Heatley, M. (1994). Neil Young. His Life and Music. London: Hamlyn.

Historical Research (21. 02 2008).

Inglis, S. (2003). Harvest. New York: Continuum.

Josephy, A. M. (1970). Red Power. US: American Heritage.

Kane, L. (2003). Ticket to Ride. Philadelphia: Running Press.

Korn, J. (1967). The Cowboys. New York: Time Life.

Korn, J. (1973). The Indians. New York: Time Life.

Krise, S. A. (08. September 2008). North American Indians in the Great War. American History .

Larimore, A. G. (1997). First Person, First Peoples. Cornell: Cornell.

Liberty, J. S. (1967). Cheyenne Memories. New Haven: Yale University press.

Lincoln, K. (1997). Native American Renaissance. Los Angeles: University of California.

Marwick, A. (1998). The Sixties. Oxford: Oxford.

McDonough, J. (2003). Shakey. London: Vintage.

Miller, D. H. (1992). Custer's Fall. The Native American Side of the Story. New York: Meridian.

Morrison, J. (1987). From Camelot to Kent State. New York: Times.

Neihardt, J. G. (1961). Black Elk Speaks. Lincoln: University of Nebraska.

Nelson, E. H. (2001). Telling Stories. US: Peter Lang.

New York Review of Books . (06. 03 2008).

Parkman, F. (1973). The Oregon Trail. London: Folio.

Petridis, A. (2000). Neil Young . Kill Your Idols. New York: Thunders Mouth Press.

Prats, A. J. (2002). Invisible Indians. Cornell: Cornell University.

Rolling Stone Magazine (1968, 1969, 1970).

Rogan, J. (1982). Neil young. London: Proteus Books.

Rogan, J. (2001). Zero to Sixty. London: Calidor.

Slotkin, R. (1998). Gunslinger Nation. Oklahoma: Oklahoma University.

Vine Deloria, J. (1988). Custer Died for your Sins. Oklahoma: University of Oklahoma.

Williamson, N. (2002). Neil Young . Journey through the Past. San Francisco: Backbeat Books.

young, N. (1974). Complete Music Vol. 1. Secaucus: Warner Bros.

Young, N. (1975). Complete Music Vol.2. Secaucus: Warner Bros.

Young, S. (2006). Neil and Me. London: McClelland & Stewart.

Films (DVDs)

BBC Documentary, (2008). Don't be Denied [Film].

BBC Documentary, (2007). Hotel California [Film].

Cash, J. (Instructor). (2000). Johnny Cash, the Man, his world, his music [Film].

Costner, K. (Instructor). (1990). Dances With Wolves [Film].

Eastwood, C. (Instructor). (1976). The Outlaw Jose Wales [Film].

Ford, J.)Instructor). (1948). Fort Apache [Film].

Ford, J. (Instructor). (1950). Rio Grande [Film].

Ford, J. (Instructor). (1949). She Wore a Yellow Ribbon [Film].

Ford, J. (Instructor). (1956). The Searchers [Film].

Forman, M. (Instructor). (1979). Hair [Film].

Jarmusch, J. (Instructor). (1995). Dead Man [Film].

Jarmusch, J. (Instructor). (1997). Year of the Horse [Film].

Nelson, R. (Instructor). (1970). Soldier Blue [Film].

Penn, A. (Instructor). (1970). Little Big Man [Film].

Young, N. (Instructor). (2006). CSNY / Deja Vu [Film].

ENDNOTES

[1] I lost my job.

[2] MA March 2009

[3] 5th November 1973. Rainbow Theatre, London, England

[4] http://en.wikipedia.org/wiki/Telstar_(song)

[5] http://en.wikipedia.org/wiki/I_Was_Lord_Kitchener's_Valet

[6] http://en.wikipedia.org/wiki/A_Taste_of_Honey

[7] http://en.wikipedia.org/wiki/Cathy_Come_Home

[8] I went on one of these marches in 1971 with my mate Barry Wood.

[9] The US versus John Lennon' David Leaf, John Scheinfeld, DVD 2006.

[10] This comes from an article in the New York Review of Books, n. 36 and is not from Dr. Brocken

[11] BBC Radio interview

[12] The Graduate, 1967 American film, directed by Mike Nichols. Based on the 1963 novel by Charles Webb.

[13] B-SIDE of 2 singles released in 1969, 'The Loner' and 'Cinnamon Girl' (1972 B-SIDE to 'heart of Gold')

[14] Neil Young and his use of Native American Imagery.

[15] Echard,2005, p.10

[16] http://en.wikipedia.org/wiki/Queen_Victoria#Later_years

[17] Name of Neil Young's cherished Gibson les Paul

[18] Yeager was reputed to have had cracked ribs when he made the flight.

[19] BBC radio interview when announcing the MA.

[20] Bloom,2001,p.145

[21] Ibid

[22] Film "Magic Trip" Alex Gibney and Alison Ellwood. 2011 (DVD)

[23] Hair (DVD)

[24] Marwick,1998,p.483

[25] Morrison,1987,p.221

[26] Rolling Stone Feb,1, 1969, p. 16

[27] Personal experience, I have personally met lots of them.

[28] http://en.wikipedia.org/wiki/1968_Olympics_Black_Power_salute

[29] Neil is vegetarian.

[30] Notes 'Reflections' [Box set] Rhino 2009

[31] Rolling Stone,1969,sept.20,p.16

[32] A song by Pete Seeger

[33]
http://www.time.com/time/magazine/article/0,9171,873851,00.html#ixzz1Mb
E7bBrq

[34] http://en.wikipedia.org/wiki/Howl

[35] http://www2.lib.virginia.edu/exhibits/sixties/leary.html

[36] Marwick,1998,p.59

[37] Josephy,1971,p.239

[38] http://da.wikipedia.org/wiki/Little_Red_Rooster

[39] Slotkin,1998,p.629

[40] Ibid,p.561

[41] www.allmovie.com

[42] Hobsbawm, 1997, p.105

[43] Marwick, 1997, p.457

[44] Kane p.271

[45] Ibid.

[46] http://en.wikipedia.org/wiki/Peter_O%27Toole

[47] Germany was divided into East Germany (DDR) and West Germany (BRD) after WW2

[48] See Beatles early interviews on YouTube.

[49] http://en.wikipedia.org/wiki/I_Wanna_Be_Your_Man

[50] FIND INFO DATE ??????

[51] Kane p.221

[52] Charles R. Cross, Room full of mirrors, p. 4

[53] http://en.wikiquote.org/wiki/A_Hard_Day's_Night_(film)

[54] See the semi documentary film 'Nowhere boy'.

[55] Bill Wyman Blues Odyssey DVD

[56] Don't Look back

[57] Charlie is My Darling

[58] House of Mirrors. Book

[59] BBC Documentary, 2008, "Hotel California"

[60] from the Neil Young album Reactor

[61] Slotkin,1998,p.340

[62] http://www.southernnewmexico.com/Articles/People/Geronimossurrender-Skelet.html

[63] Sleeve notes CD 'The Great Elvis Presley, The Hayride Shows'

[64] http://en.wikipedia.org/wiki/Patsy_Cline's_Greatest_Hits

[65] Alan Clayson, p.20

[66] Alan Clayson, p.30

[67] The Word,aug.09,issue 78,p.83

[68] Johnny Cash sings ballads of The True West. Bitter Tears.

[69] Liner notes to 'Bitter Tears' by Hugh Cherry.

[70] Section 34, Grave 479A

[71] Cheewa, p.138

[72] http://www.runningpast.com/billy_mills.htm

[73] Soundtrack of the film "Lone Star"

[74] http://en.wikipedia.org/wiki/Lovesick_Blues

[75] DVD,2008, Heart of Gold

[76] BBC documentary 'Don't be Denied'

[77] Radio Jazz (Copenhagen.)

[78] Life' Neil Young and Crazy Horse 1987

[79] See sources Mazzeo,

[80] P.5 Oxford Companion to Film, Oxford University Press London 1976

[81] Geoff Emerick did this and was later reprimanded by management

[82] Invented by EMI engineer Ken Townsend in 1966, to create doubled vocal track.

[83] www.bobdylan.com/#/songs/talkin-world-war-III-blues

[84] BBC,2206, Hotel California.

[85] DVD, http://www.amazon.co.uk/CSNY-Deja-DVD-David-Crosby/dp/B001CD3P92

[86] A Long Time Gone, introduction

[87] http://www.thrasherswheat.org/fot/ohio.htm

[88] http://video.google.com/videoplay?docid=-3727445416544720642#docid=2037044267667802683

[89] Notes to David Crosby's 'Voyager' CD box.

[90] Popular Book and Film in the fifties 'The man in the Grey Flannel Suit' (1955) by Sloan Wilson.

[91] Morrison,1987,p.159

[92] Marwick,1998,p.483

[93] Kellogg's family had a house on Saltspring Island, BC, Canada, they seldom had time to use.

[94] Marwick,1998,p.483

[95] The Police Regatta De Blanc

[96] American Forces Network

[97] These broadcast from just outside English waters.

[98] http://www.bbc.co.uk/totp2/trivia/pans_people/ruth_pearson/page1.shtml

[99] Personal memory

[100] http://en.wikipedia.org/wiki/Heart_of_Gold_(song)

[101] See Lynne, Rusties second letter. (Part two of the Hippie trilogy)

[102] The book: When Giants walked the earth.

[103] www.BBC.co.uk

[104] Slotkin, 1998,p.589

[105] Wikipedia

[106] Krouse, 2008,p.575

[107] It is believed to be a military veterinarians jacket.

[108] Slotkin. P.629

[109] Gallop, 2001,p.39

[110] Time life,1973,p.209

[111] Gallop,2002,p.19

[112] Gallop,2002,p.117

[113] Gallop,2001,p.99

[114] Slotkin,1998,p.87

[115] Zane,1956 P.64

[116] Life Magazine The First Fifty Years, p. 221

[117] 114 Slotkin,1998,p.630

[118] Gallop 2001,p98

[119] Havighurst, p.119

[120] Furay, 1997,p.270

[121] Rogan2001,p.354

[122] Extra material with the DVD box set.

[123] The Beatles Interviews 2(CD, Newsound 200)

[124] Rolling Stone, 2003, Sep.4, p.4

[125] Slotkin,1998,p.349

[126] Wild West Shows. L.G.Moses, P.230.

[127] ibid, P.231.

[128] Slotkin, Gunslinger Nation, p. 629

[129] http://www.astonisher.com/archives/museum/crazy_horse_surrender.html

[130] www.allmovieguide.com

[131] Searchers DVD collector's edition, extra material.

[132] Slotkin, 1998, p. 259

[133] Slotkin , 1998, p.631

[134] Personal experience, I heard this from a Scottish guy I worked with called John who was in the cinema.

[135] Wikipedia

[136] Rolling Stone, 1970,March 19,p.44

[137] BBC, The My Lai Tapes[61] on Radio 4, March 15, 2008

[138] New Riders of the Purple Sage, Eagles

[139] Allmovieguide.com

[140] Slotkin ,1998,p.630

[141] Prat, 2002, p.132-133

[142] Prat, 2002, p. 259

[143] Elliott,2007,p.3

[144] Prat, 2002, p.258

[145] Slotkin 1998,p.76

[146] Prat, 2002, p.179

[147] NY Review, March 2008, p.29

[148] Notes from Turtle Island.

[149] Forbis, 1972, p.93

[150] Martinguitar.com

[151] Slotkin p. 260

[152] www.allmusicguide.com

[153] http://www.creative-native.com/lyrics/soldier.htm

[154] Bloom, 2001,p.5

[155] Cobb,2007,p.144

[156] Morrison, 1987, p.76-77

[157] Marwick, 1997, p. 535

[158] Morrison, 1987, p.19

[159] Slotkin,1998, p. 524

[160] Marwick, 1998,p.560

[161] Deloria, 1988,p.10

[162] Cobb, 2007,p.5

[163] Josephy, 1971

[164] Slotkin, 1998, p.629

[165] Josephy, 1971,p.3

[166] Fixico

[167] Ibid,p.222

[168] Ibid,p.233

[169] Cobb,2007,p.5

[170] Cobb,2007,p.5

[171] Josephy,1971, p.5

[172] Josephy,1971,p.238

[173] DVD, 1969, Johnny Cash, the man, his world, his music

[174] Johnny Cash would later drop his claim on Cherokee blood.

[175] Josephy,1971,p.185

[176] http://en.wikipedia.org/wiki/Redbone_(band)

[177] Cobb,2007,p.14

[178] Ibid, p.14

[179] Deloria, 1988,p.4

[180] Morrison, 1987,p.159

[181] US National Park Service (nps.gov)

[182] Furay,1997,p.255

ABOUT THE AUTHOR

Stephen M. Catchpole was born within the sound of the Bow Bells.

He grew up in Camberley, Surrey. He went on the road in 1972 and during the next four years travelled extensively in Europe, North Africa and Canada..

He works as a teacher and has two sons. He has an MA in Social Studies from University of North London and a Cand.mag in History from the University of Copenhagen.

www.ingramcontent.com/pod-product-compliance
Lightning Source LLC
Chambersburg PA
CBHW032035040426
42449CB00007B/897